from Research to the Music Classroom

3459

Music and Students at Risk: Creative Solutions for a National Dilemma

Jack A. Taylor, Nancy H. Barry, and Kimberly C. Walls

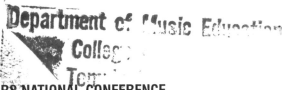

Department of Music Education
College
Tem

MUSIC EDUCATORS NATIONAL CONFERENCE

Contents

Foreword

More than twenty years have elapsed since the publication of the first monographs in the MENC series *From Research to the Music Classroom*. In the foreword to that original series, it was noted that "research, even with all of its frailties, is the best way mankind has yet devised for unearthing objective truth." In the intervening twenty years, research in all fields of human endeavor has expanded enormously. While it may be debatable as to whether mankind is now any closer to unearthing "objective truth," it is indisputable that in the past twenty years we have witnessed an unparalleled knowledge explosion. It is that knowledge explosion, especially in the area of music teaching and learning, that makes the publication of this new *From Research to the Music Classroom* series so important.

The purpose of each book in this series is threefold:

- to identify specific topics of interest to music teachers at all levels
- to summarize and synthesize all the research that has been done related to the specific topic
- to draw some tentative conclusions based on the research and to make some practical suggestions for music teachers.

Research findings can be an invaluable resource for music teachers at all levels. One word of caution is necessary, however. Research is a continuing process and as new evidence emerges and old evidence is reinterpreted, beliefs and conclusions must be adjusted accordingly. Research findings are rarely applicable in all teaching situations, and sound judgment must be used in interpreting those findings. Research, however, can provide direction for music teachers interested in evaluating and updating their teaching on a regular basis. It is that ideal to which this series is dedicated.

—Charles A. Elliott
Series Editor
From Research to the Music Classroom

Preface

This book represents six years of research into one of the most pressing problems in our society today—students at risk—and how the arts can help. Behavior and conditions that define a child as "at risk" are part of a self-perpetuating cycle of failure across generations, a cycle of failure that often manifests itself through school dropouts. Participation in the arts in school can help at-risk youth break this cycle. The arts contribute something to the school-day environment other subjects cannot. This "something," coupled with successful experiences in the arts, can encourage youth to stay in school and to succeed in other academic areas. By staying in school, at-risk students may have access to badly needed social services that are more difficult to obtain outside the school setting.

Six years of research have convinced us that music and the arts really can make a difference in the lives of at-risk students and that those special qualities inherent in arts experiences can be very useful for intervention with troubled youth. All music and arts teachers should be aware of the research literature that points out the benefits of arts experiences. Because of the proliferation of problems throughout society, we must assume that all teachers will be faced with the challenge of motivating and educating at-risk youngsters. It is essential, therefore, that music teachers equip themselves with an arsenal of proactive teaching strategies, both from arts and nonarts programs, to use in their own teaching.

The authors prepared this document to provide teachers with an overview of the at-risk phenomenon in the United States and to acquaint teachers with ways that the arts can be used for prevention and intervention. Our research and recommendations for ways that music teachers can address the needs of at-risk students (see Chapter 6) are based upon a variety of sources: published and unpublished literature, newspaper clippings, written surveys, interviews, and many telephone calls to follow up on tips about unadvertised programs dealing with at-risk students. In the course of our investigation, we encountered many publications, which, while useful for promoting the arts in schools, asserted benefits of music and arts education unsubstantiated by disciplined inquiry. Those documents are not cited here, nor did they influence our conclusions and recommendations.

We analyzed a large body of research regarding at-risk children and a great number of at-risk programs, but we realize that our work is not exhaustive. Even as you are reading this, more research is underway, and other at-risk programs are being initiated. We expect that the results of these efforts will confirm and complement our findings, and we encourage the reader to continually seek out these new sources of information.

In this book, we first present the problem, showing how the danger of dropping out of school can have crippling consequences on society; then, we describe briefly the positive role that music educators can play on this negative "stage" (Chapter 1). In Chapter 2, we define risk in general terms and also as it is observed in school settings. Our aim in the first part of the chapter is to get our readers familiar with this problem, so that in the second part of the chapter the descriptions of high-risk behaviors and early warning signs will help readers to identify young people who may be at risk. Chapter 3 is a survey of ways that have been shown to help students who are potential school dropouts and contains programs and ideas that can be incorporated into any school curriculum. We proceed to narratives of special music and other arts programs in Chapter 4. These special curricula, partnerships, case studies, and so on are not restricted to specific geographic locations. As you will see, they are scattered across the United States. They reach out to any student in need, regardless of race or economic status. Our purpose is to show that through music and the other arts, caring teachers, school administrators, parents, and community volunteers are making a difference in the lives of young people who would otherwise be cast off by society. As a way of emphasizing the power of the arts to motivate and inspire young people (and in many ways a continuation of Chapter 4), Chapter 5 presents perspectives from four respected music educators and a group of elementary school music teachers. These people draw upon their experiences with at-risk music students and describe both the rationale and capacity of music to inspire and motivate young people. In Chapter 6, we have attempted to pull together our personal observations and readings about at-risk students. We believe that the conclusions in this chapter are noteworthy and are, at the very least, topics that must be considered by teachers who are concerned about the welfare of students who may be heading down a disastrous path. Finally, for the interest of our readers (and for those who choose to do research), an annotated bibliography on the topics of at-risk students, dropout prevention, and the arts concludes this document. We do not claim that it is complete; in fact, we know that it is just a sample of the fine work undertaken in this important area.

We should add one final disclaimer. This document does not include descriptions of all music or arts programs that serve students at risk. Ongoing programs are not always well advertised; thus, it is not easy to locate the ones that have not been publicized (in newspapers, magazines, or on television). We do feel, however, that the programs described here are representative of a broad variety of solutions to the at-risk problem; thus, we have confidence in our conclusions and recommendations.

The authors would appreciate hearing from readers who know of, or are involved in, current at-risk and dropout programs in music and the other arts. Please contact us at the address below.

Jack A. Taylor
Center for Music Research
214 KMU, Drawer AR
Florida State University
Tallahassee, FL 32306-2098
Telephone: 904-644-5785
Fax: 904-644-6100
E-mail: *taylor@cmr.fsu.edu*

Chapter 1

A National Dilemma

At-risk students are children or adolescents who are unlikely to become responsible, contributing members of society due to delinquency, substance abuse, teen pregnancy, school failure, or suicide (Davis & McCaul, 1990; Dryfoos, 1990). They are "children who hurt, physically or psychologically, and children who have problems—educational problems, personal problems, or social problems" (Frymier, 1992, p. v). Statistics reported by Peter Scales, executive director of the Anchorage Center for Families, attest to the severity of the problem:

- Every 31 seconds, a teenager becomes pregnant.
- Every two minutes, a teenager gives birth.
- Every 78 seconds, an adolescent attempts suicide.
- Every 20 minutes, an adolescent dies in an accident of some kind.
- Approximately every 1 to 1.5 hours, one teenager is murdered and another commits suicide.
- By age 18, 1 in 4 girls and 1 in 10 boys are sexually abused.
- By age 18, 1 in 8 teenagers will run away from home at least once (Crutsinger, 1991, p. 29).

Furthermore, the U.S. Center for Disease Control reported that every day in 1990, 11 adolescents from the ages of 15–19 were killed by guns (Center for Disease Control, 1993). In 1992, child abuse killed 1261 children (National Committee for Child Abuse, 1993).

When we examine current statistics on the prevalence of at-risk characteristics and behaviors among our youth, it becomes evident that most music teachers certainly will encounter at-risk students in their classes. At-risk students present challenges for educators, who sometimes view them as negative influences in the music classroom. Nevertheless, at-risk students should be encouraged to participate in music and arts classes. Music teachers are in a unique position to reach out to these students, because music and other arts classes can provide students with an intellectually and emotionally nourishing environment that may not be available in other courses. Music and the arts offer students a way to express themselves and to take pride in individual accomplishment. Participation in performing ensembles gives them an opportunity to be part of a group and helps develop a sense of belonging. MENC acknowledges the importance of serving at-risk students in the music class in paragraph 49 of the MENC Statement of Beliefs: "The Music Educators National Conference recognizes that increased efforts are necessary to meet the musical needs of students with disabilities, at-risk students, and students who are gifted and talented in music" (MENC, 1991, p. 3).

Teachers often become aware that a student is at risk when the student's problems are manifested through "acting-out" behaviors. These acting-out behaviors are frequently associated with delinquency. Delinquency can refer to a wide variety of socially unacceptable behaviors ranging from mild acting-out incidents to violent criminal offenses. The Federal Bureau of Investigation categorizes criminal offenses such as robbery, aggravated assault, rape, and homicide as "index offenses" because these acts are not age related, while offenses associated with youth such as running away from home, truancy, and under-age drinking are classified as "status offenses" (Dryfoos, 1990).

At-risk behaviors and their accompanying antecedents are closely associated with dropping out of school. Educators throughout the nation are urgently addressing the problem of how to encourage students to stay in school until graduation. It is commonly agreed that a large portion of America's youth are at risk for dropping out of school, but it is impossible to specify the exact number today because of the difficulties of tracking America's transient students and the different methods of calculating dropout statistics. Nevertheless, a current estimate of the problem states that about one-third of American children are at risk of dropping out of school (Brodinsky & Keough, 1989; McCormick, 1989). Dropout rates in several large cities are much higher (Grossnickle, 1986), with national rates for some minorities topping 80% ("The State Plan to Reduce the Dropout Rate," 1991). About 381,000 students dropped out of school in 1993 (Schwartz, 1995). Two of the strongest predictors of dropping out are (1) having low grades and (2) being behind modal grade (the grade level appropriate to the student's age). Recent statistics indicate that 27% of our teenagers are behind modal grade (Dryfoos, 1990). The dropout rate is 70% for students kept back once and increases to 90% for students kept back twice (Ratliff, 1991). The situation seems to be getting worse: The dropout rate in the year 2000 is projected to be 40% (West Virginia School Dropout Prevention Task Force, 1991).

We all pay the price

Dropping out of school can be devastating for both the student and society. Dropouts have lower earnings than high school graduates and face other economic disadvantages. With fewer employment and advancement opportunities, dropouts make 30% less in lifetime earnings than do high school graduates. In dollars, that translates to about $212,000 less (Brodinsky & Keough, 1989; Schwartz, 1995; Spencer & Bearden, 1987; West Virginia School Dropout Prevention Task Force, 1991). On the average, nongraduates have retirement incomes that are half that of graduates' incomes (West Virginia School Dropout Prevention Task Force, 1991). Almost one-half of welfare families' heads of households are dropouts (Schwartz, 1995).

At-risk behaviors in American society continue to rise, with 41% of the population having no high school diploma (Brodinsky & Keough, 1989). Each dropout cost society $8,244 in lost earnings and taxes in 1986 (Patton et al, 1991). The dropouts from the class of 1991 will cost Americans $238,000,000 in lost earnings and $68,000,000 in lost taxes. The accompanying rises in the costs of welfare and unemployment programs further reduce the amount of funds available for education and dropout prevention. Dropouts often suffer from a diminished sense of worth and personal satisfaction, thus creating stress, high blood pressure, and heart attacks. The result is job absenteeism and ultimately higher health insurance costs for everyone (West Virginia School Dropout Prevention Task Force, 1991).

The manifold costs of at-risk behaviors

Our prisons are overpopulated with adults who have been juvenile delinquents, substance abusers, or school failures (Schwartz, 1995). Dropouts are six to ten times more likely to be involved in crime than are high school graduates. Between 70–90% of prison inmates as well as about 75% of juvenile delinquents are dropouts (Grossnickle, 1986; West Virginia School Dropout Prevention Task Force, 1991). Teen pregnancies often produce children who are susceptible to health-related learning disabilities, thus perpetuating the cycle of school failure and dropping out (Dryfoos, 1990).

The role of the music educator

Music educators must be involved with at-risk intervention. Successful at-risk intervention programs must permeate *all* areas of the school environment (including music and arts classes). Successful programs must begin in the early grades and extend through high school graduation. Music classes offer unique learning experiences that help some at-risk students maintain interest in school, increase self-esteem, and foster a sense of belonging. Opportunities for hands-on participation and self-expression associated with music and other arts can be more gratifying and inherently motivating than the experiences associated with other courses. Music activities can reinforce learning in other disciplines (such as learning scientific concepts by constructing simple percussion instruments, developing language arts skills through song-writing activities, and so on) (Barry, 1996).

Music teachers can make a difference. Many students report that their sole reason for staying in school (and out of trouble) was the motivation and inspiration derived from participation in the arts. Students often cite their relationship with their arts teacher as the one thing that carried them through the rough times. At-risk students can be successful in music and contribute to the music-learning experiences of other students. As their musical success—and thus their importance to the ensemble—increases, their self-esteem also grows. A taste of success may motivate students to succeed in other content areas, to stay in school, and to graduate.

There have not been many objective studies of *how* music and the arts help in at-risk intervention, but several at-risk programs have included the arts. Music educators can help their students by being aware of who is at risk and adopting some of the successful strategies used in at-risk intervention programs, even those that do not include the arts.

Summary

American children are at risk in many ways. Legions of students across the country are victims of circumstances that place them at risk, and many are engaged in dangerous and destructive behaviors. This problem permeates and affects all facets of society. As citizens, taxpayers, parents, and teachers, we all pay the price!

The problem is serious, but not hopeless. Teachers, working with the support of the community, can make a difference. Music and arts teachers are in a unique position to help at-risk students because of the satisfaction that many students find in participation in arts activities, in the camaraderie derived from creative group efforts, and in the unique opportunity for self-expression through the arts.

Chapter 2

Students at Risk

Defining "at risk"

The term "at risk" appears frequently in educational literature. Students can be at risk in a number of ways; for example, students can be at risk of not completing their education. When students have experienced little success or gratification in school, the prospect of "dropping out" may seem all too inviting. Students can also be at risk of alcohol or drug addiction as a way to escape from problems and frustrations. Students can be at risk of becoming parents before they become adults: As Dougherty states, "Becoming pregnant proves that for a little while you were of some value to someone" (Dougherty, 1990, p. 7). Students can also be at risk of becoming involved in gangs and criminal activity—a sense of group identity and belonging can be a powerful incentive. Sometimes, when the apathy and frustration become too much to bear, students can be at risk of ending their lives (Dryfoos, 1990).

A student must remain "within the system" to have access to special programs, facilities, and much-needed support from caring adults. For that reason, controlling the dropout problem is a key element in the struggle to remediate the circumstances that place a student at risk. Social workers, parole officers, and other professionals certainly attempt to maintain contact and continue positive interactions with the dropout, but consistent contact with these professionals is assured only if the student remains within the school environment. Disliking school is the reason students give most frequently for dropping out (Garibaldi & Bartley, 1987); ironically, the at-risk student's best (and perhaps only) chance of breaking the vicious cycle of frustration and failure is to stay in school. Successful partic- ipation in music and other arts activities contributes to increased self-esteem and a greater sense of belonging within the school environment. In fact, the only reason many students choose to remain in school is because of their involvement in the arts (e.g., Barry, Taylor, & Walls, 1990; Modugno, 1991). It is important for music teachers to acknowledge this fact and to take on the challenging task of helping to make a difference in at-risk students' lives through music.

To provide services to those students most in need, teach- ers must be aware of the circumstances and situations that place students at risk. There have been many attempts to pro- file the at-risk student, but it is not always possible to predict which students eventually will experience problems within school and society. In 1988, Jennings reported that 25 states had formal definitions of at-risk students, but in most instances, definitions of at-risk students are a matter of legisla- tion and local politics. The length and complexity of lists of indicators vary from school system to school system (Dougherty, 1990; Morris & Schultz, eds., 1991). Certainly, almost every student is at risk to some degree, but there are particular circumstances and behaviors that tend to place some students in a "high risk" category. These risk indicators are divided into two categories: (1) descriptive characteristics or "antecedent" circumstances that place students at risk, and (2) "high-risk behaviors" in which the at-risk tendency becomes manifested and compounded when the student encounters problems within the school and society (Dryfoos, 1990).

Descriptive characteristics

Certain characteristics and situations tend to place students at risk. This does not mean that every student with one or more of these characteristics will eventually experience serious difficulties, but it does suggest that these students may face a greater probability of encountering problems that lead to their decline. It is also important to note that the same at-risk factor may appear for different reasons, as shown in the following example:

> One child may get poor grades ... because he failed to learn to read well. Another child may get poor grades because his parents do not value education and they never encourage him to do so, nor help him with his homework. Still another child may get poor grades because his peers press him to hang around or do drugs that divert his attention from learning, or because his neurological apparatus makes it difficult to relate incoming stimuli to previous experience. In other words, even when the risk indicator shows up the same way—poor grades—the indicator is only a symptom of the problem, not the problem itself. (Frymier, 1992, p. 50)

The following list is not exhaustive, but it does reflect characteristics consistently cited in the literature as part of the profile of the at-risk student:

- Gender influences the types of high-risk behaviors that students exhibit. Males are more likely to drop out of school (Presseisen, 1988) and to commit acts of violence and aggression. Females are at risk of becoming pregnant and have a greater tendency toward suicide than males (e.g., Dryfoos, 1990; McArthur, 1986; Spencer & Bearden, 1987).

- Low socioeconomic level can have a negative impact on many aspects of a child's life (e.g., Dropout Prevention, 1989; Jurgens, 1985; Spencer & Bearden, 1987; Strother, 1987; United States General Accounting Office [USGAO], 1987). Poverty-stricken children are faced with disadvantages and situations that children from more privileged environments usually do not have to endure. Some researchers cite poverty as the most powerful predictor of students who eventually engage in high-risk behavior (Dryfoos, 1990; Garibaldi & Bartley, 1987). These problems tend to become even more pronounced among the homeless and those individuals living in shelters (Schwartz, 1995).

- A history of low grades and lack of success in school, especially when the student has been kept back for one or

more grade levels, can contribute to low self-esteem and
lack of motivation (e.g., Dougherty, 1990; Dropout
Prevention, 1989; Garibaldi & Bartley, 1987; Watson,
1991). Why should a student choose to remain within an
environment in which he or she experiences little or no
success? School failure and low academic achievement are
frequently cited as the strongest predictors of students who
will eventually drop out of school (e.g., Cheshire, 1991;
Dropout Prevention, 1989; Schwartz, 1995; Spencer &
Bearden, 1987; United States General Accounting Office
[USGAO], 1987; Wilcynski, 1987).

- Low academic skills, especially reading, if not remediated,
are early indicators of students who may experience
increasingly greater difficulties within the school environment (e.g., Dougherty, 1990; Grossnickle, 1986;
Middleton, 1980; Presseisen, 1988; Ratliff, 1991).

- Students who prefer work to school may not be motivated
to achieve academic success. For a youngster, the immediate and very tangible benefits of a paycheck may outweigh
the potential benefits of an education (e.g., Garibaldi &
Bartley, 1987; Spencer & Bearden, 1987; USGAO, 1987).

- Students who have siblings, other close relatives, or friends
who have dropped out of school are more likely to experience difficulties within the school environment and to
eventually drop out themselves (e.g., Dropout Prevention,
1989; Grossnickle, 1986; Ratliff, 1991; Schwartz, 1995).

- Students in families in which one or both parents have
dropped out of school are more prone to problems in
school and tend to be at greater risk of dropping out than
students whose parents completed high school (e.g.,
USGAO, 1987; Grossnickle, 1986).

- Problems at home ranging from dysfunctional family situations to emotional and/or physical abuse can cause students to be at risk. Living in a stressful home environment
has been associated with many high-risk behaviors,
including depression and emotional problems, truancy and
tardiness, delinquency and acting out, sexual promiscuity,
substance abuse, school failure and dropping out (e.g.,
Dougherty, 1990; Ratliff, 1991; Rumberger, 1983;
Strother, 1991).

- Feelings of alienation within the school environment contribute to a lack of motivation. This factor is frequently associated with students who eventually drop out of school (e.g., Hershaff, 1978; Loken, 1973; Middleton, 1980; Presseisen, 1988; Schwartz, 1995).

- Low self-esteem contributes to self-destructive behaviors such as substance abuse and early sexual intercourse. Students with low self-esteem may lack academic motivation and may experience many school failures. Low self-esteem is also associated with student attrition (e.g., Dougherty, 1990; Grossnickle, 1986; Myles, 1984; Ratliff, 1991; Wehlage, Rutter, & Turnbaugh, 1987).

- Numerous school transfers and family moves can contribute to feelings of alienation within the school environment and can make it more difficult for a student to achieve academic success. The student may be reluctant to get involved in school clubs and activities, and therefore may fail to establish a sense of belonging. Students who perceive themselves as outsiders are more likely to engage in acting-out behaviors (e.g., Grossnickle, 1986; Strother, 1991).

High-risk behaviors

Certain high-risk behaviors have been linked with the at-risk phenomenon. These situations are ones in which the student's problems become most apparent. They reflect the at-risk tendency through attitudes, choices, and acting-out behaviors. The following situations and behaviors are often harbingers of much more severe problems:

- Delinquency and acting-out (e.g., Dryfoos, 1990; Strother, 1991; USGAO, 1987)
- Problems with faculty and adult authority figures (e.g., Cheshire, 1991; Grossnickle, 1986; Jurgens, 1985; Spencer & Bearden, 1987; USGAO, 1987)
- Expulsion or suspension from school (e.g., Garibaldi & Bartley, 1987; Spencer & Bearden, 1987; Strother, 1991; Watson, 1991)
- Substance abuse (e.g., Dryfoos, 1990; Presseisen, 1988)
- Lack of involvement in school activities (e.g., Cheshire,

1991; Dougherty, 1990; Garibaldi & Bartley, 1987; Jurgens, 1985; Loken, 1973)

- Unprotected intercourse at an early age (e.g., Dryfoos, 1990; Strother, 1991)
- Pregnancy (e.g., Garibaldi & Bartley, 1987; Rumberger, 1983; Spencer & Bearden, 1987; USGAO, 1987)
- Truancy and tardiness (e.g, Cheshire, 1991; Dougherty, 1990; Dryfoos, 1990; USGAO, 1987)
- School failure and dropping out (e.g., Dryfoos, 1990; Franklin & Streeter, 1995; USGAO, 1987; Watson, 1991; Wilson, 1985)

Risk tends to be pervasive. High-risk behaviors are often associated with circumstances beyond the child's control, such as being economically or socially disadvantaged. Whenever one type of risk factor is present in a child's life, it is usually accompanied by other risk factors (Franklin & Streeter, 1995; Frymier, 1992). Teachers are painfully aware that most of the risk factors in a child's life are beyond the control of the school. The odds may seem overwhelming, but teachers can still make a difference in the lives of troubled young people.

Early warning signs

Students do not suddenly become at risk when they reach adolescence, although high-risk behaviors are most noticeable in the teenage years. The chain of events that ultimately places a child at risk frequently begins at a very early age (e.g., Gudeman, 1987; Middleton, 1980; Strother, 1991; Wilcynski, 1987). "Like the decision to use drugs, the decision to drop out of school is usually made in the fourth and fifth grades, making early intervention essential" (Ratliff, 1991, p. 126).

According to a recent report from the Missouri Department of Elementary and Secondary Education, the following "indicators of potential dropouts … are reliable predictors as early as elementary school" (Dougherty, 1990):

- High absentee rate
- High truancy rate
- Low academic skills or aptitude, including low grades, weak reading skills, low test scores and academic deficiencies, or a history of failure/being held back in school
- Referrals for social work or psychological assistance

- Recurring discipline problems
- Rebellious attitude/inability to relate to authority
- A low-income family
- A poorly educated mother
- A fatherless home
- A parent or sibling who dropped out of school
- Low self-esteem (p. 12).

The reasons for students becoming truly at risk are myriad. Data that are very accurate from a perspective of group dynamics can become misleading when applied to an individual situation. Anytime checklists and criteria are used to diagnose a problem as vast and complex as the at-risk phenomenon there is always the danger of attaching an undeserved label to one student, while simultaneously overlooking (and denying needed services to) another student. Checklists and profiles are most useful as general guidelines for detecting the warning signs that can alert the educator to potential problems. It is important to remember that whether or not an individual student is at risk can be determined only through careful observation. Some researchers are using the results of individual case studies to provide insight into the circumstances that place a child at risk (e.g., Grossnickle, 1986; Strother, 1991). Educators must remember that caring, concern, and communication at an individual level are essential for developing profiles of the student at risk.

Summary

Students are at risk for a number of different reasons. Because each situation is unique, it is impossible to provide a profile of the typical at-risk student. It is important, however, for parents and educators to be aware of the warning signs. These warning signs fall into two categories: (1) descriptive characteristics and (2) high-risk behaviors. While the most severe, high-risk behaviors may not be evident until adolescence, a number of early warning signs have been identified. Since early intervention is critical, these warning signs can be especially useful to both parents and educators.

Chapter 3

Successful Strategies, Ideas, and Programs in Other Disciplines

What works?

Music programs are not immune from the troubling issues that permeate the school environment. All educators must be concerned about these problems, but arts teachers are in a unique position to make a difference in the lives of troubled students. There is evidence that the arts can have a positive influence upon at-risk students, but at this time, the majority of intervention programs for at-risk students have been conducted in other disciplines. It is important, therefore, for arts educators to study intervention programs in nonarts areas to learn about ways to address at-risk student needs.

Over the past several years, a number of schools throughout the nation have implemented intervention programs for at-risk students. Grossnickle (1986) summarizes the approaches commonly used by these schools:

- Adopting and enforcing attendance and truancy policies
- Providing tutorial assistance and opportunities to make up work
- Providing early identification and remediation of academic failures
- Expanding special services such as school social workers
- Offering vocational and work-study programs
- Providing homebound tutoring for pregnant students
- Providing reading-improvement labs and individualized and computer-assisted instruction
- Establishing alternative schools
- Providing special in-service workshops for teachers on dealing with at-risk students
- Working with police on gang activity
- Establishing articulation with feeder schools
- Establishing peer counseling programs
- Providing night school and summer remediation programs (pp. 15–16).

Each community is unique. Grossnickle (1986) points out that to be effective, a dropout prevention program must address local needs and problems. He recommends the following steps for planning a comprehensive program:

- Adopt a schoolwide philosophy promoting a positive learning environment ensuring student success.
- Analyze dropout statistics and identify major reasons why students drop out.
- Implement a preventive dropout program that provides early identification of high-risk students.
- Train teachers, counselors, and other school personnel in effective intervention strategies.
- Identify resources in the school and community that can be used to help students with special needs and problems (p. 16).

Individualization

One of the keys to successful dropout prevention is individualized attention and instruction (Keller et al., 1991). Furthermore, program sites should be organized to empower principals and teachers to meet their students' individual needs (Altieri, 1991; Levin, 1987; The State Plan, 1991; Wehlage,

Lipman, & Smith, 1989). Effective programs use a variety of gender- and culture-sensitive strategies (Diem, 1991). Smaller schools and smaller classes help individualize services for at-risk students (Bass, 1991; The State Plan, 1991). School personnel, parents, and students work together to create an atmosphere of concern for the individual by developing and implementing rules for behavior (Damico & Roth, 1991).

I-CANN (Individualized Course Alternative, Now or Never) is one of several programs at Hazelwood Junior High School in Florissant, Missouri. It was designed for students who "fall through the cracks"—those individuals of average intelligence who still exhibit disruptive behavior and who fail or barely pass. I-CANN is a time-out program that removes students from the regular classroom and places them in smaller group settings where they have an opportunity to discuss their problems. Counseling, as well as academics, is an important part of the program. I-CANN students have a close working relationship with an adult. Individual parent/teacher conferences and positive group meetings encourage parental support and involvement. I-CANN students work cooperatively on hands-on projects.

> "All I-CANN classes have an academic focus developed around a series of meaningful projects. The small class size, the relaxed atmosphere, and treating kids as worthy and capable of making a contribution created a climate that allowed them to learn skills and content as well as grow in stature in their own eyes and those of their peers." (Dougherty, 1990, p. 30)

High expectations

Effective programs maintain high expectations for students (Conrath, 1989; West Virginia School Dropout Prevention Task Force, 1991). Fruitful interventions are academically rigorous and include a variety of subjects. In productive programs, students take responsibility for their learning and their behavior, often participating in cooperative learning, team learning, and/or peer tutoring (Meyer, Harootunian, William, & Steinberg, 1991; Thompson, 1991). Ability grouping and tracking tend to defeat efforts to build self-esteem, responsibility, and the motivation to succeed.

Early intervention

The most effective dropout prevention begins early, even before birth, and is long term and comprehensive (Altieri,

1991). Longitudinal studies of programs such as Head Start indicate that direct instruction and positive reinforcement can contribute to lower grade retention rates, higher attendance, and higher graduation rates (Stallings, 1987). Family involvement is a crucial component of early intervention. It is essential to establish communication between families and service providers. In addition, families must be included in decision making (Rosenkoetter & Shotts, 1994; Stief, 1994). Young children require special attention during points of transition between services and settings. The increased emphasis upon academics in kindergarten forces young children to experience failures that may compromise future school success. The transition from preschool to kindergarten, therefore, requires special attention (Stief, 1994).

Parental involvement

Although very few school programs have had full parent participation, the emphasis of some successful programs is the teaching of parenting skills. Union County Middle School in the "economically depressed northeast, Appalachian area of Georgia" (Ensley, McGuire, Moose, & Everett, 1991, p. 221) made communication and interaction with parents a priority. In an attempt to alleviate a traditionally high dropout rate (around 40%), the middle school implemented several programs directed toward at-risk students. A special team of teachers was selected and trained to interact with at-risk students and their parents. Team members used communication strategies such as personal invitations to the school's open house, home visits, sharing family crises, regular written communications with parents, open home telephone policy (parents and teachers call each other at home to discuss their concerns about students), and scheduling personal conferences at the parents' convenience.

Good ideas do not always work. The NoFAIL (Necessary For All Individuals to Learn) program at Hazelwood Junior High School in Missouri was based upon three premises that in order for students to succeed, the school must (1) teach study skills, develop student self-discipline, and provide motivation; (2) assist parents in helping their children become better students; and (3) provide supervision of homework and study skills when parents cannot or will not provide it. The program began in the fall of 1985 with a grant from the

Danforth Foundation. The program focused on teaching students skills in studying, test taking, time management and other organizational tools. Students identified by the school staff were scheduled for after-school sessions two days a week. The ambitious program was very flexible, allowing time for participation in after-school clubs and sports. Nevertheless, it was not successful. Students resented having to attend more school and were not motivated.

The NoFAIL program was a good idea, but it overlooked two important elements: students and parents. Without student motivation and parental support, the vital study skills that NoFAIL attempted to teach were not learned. Hazelwood faculty developed a second program to replace the unsuccessful NoFAIL—the OK Club. The OK Club (Opportunity Knocks or Outstanding Kids) retained the emphasis on developing study skills; but unlike NoFAIL, this program also emphasized self-esteem and motivation. The OK Club also encouraged parental support and involvement through monthly meetings. Student membership in the OK Club depended upon parent attendance at the meetings. Students were frequently reminded to ask their parents to attend, invitations were sent, and phone calls were made. The OK Club parent meetings eventually evolved into a "support group for parents who previously had been frustrated by their inability to help their children succeed in school and who thought they were the only ones having the problem" (Dougherty, 1990, p. 18).

Motivation

Students need reasons for staying in school, and there are ways to motivate them to do so. "School must be a place that is exciting and enticing. Nontraditional activities must be coupled with traditional activities to provide experiences outside the realm of the classroom" (Deaton & Blair, 1991, p. 159). At West Forest Elementary School, an innovative "school of the future" in Lee County, Alabama, students are encouraged to learn through a variety of creative hands-on experiences. "American Heritage Week" is an example of this type of integrated learning. Each grade level is assigned a particular historical period which is developed through a four-week multidisciplinary unit culminating in a five-day extravaganza.

"Students demonstrate their knowledge [of the historical period] by presenting skits, reciting poetry, singing, performing dances, and displaying arts and crafts characteristic of the assigned time period ... As a finale, a Village Fair featuring early American crafts and games is held. Tents are pitched on the school grounds under which local artisans and craftsmen exhibit blacksmithing, roping, scrimshaw, macrame, folk art, woodcutting, stenciling, butter churning, quilting, basketry, pottery making, and embroidery." (Deaton & Blair, 1991, p. 60)

Not all intervention programs are successful. Negative strategies such as raising graduation requirements and ability tracking can lead to increased dropout rates (Dryfoos, 1990). Although well-intentioned, plans that deny at-risk students access to extracurricular activities and arts programs often function as punitive. In some cases, at-risk students are automatically assigned into schedules of remedial academics and vocational subjects with no time for the fine arts. Some at-risk elementary students must give up music time for academic remediation or social services. Increased graduation requirements have resulted in more high school dropouts as well as smaller music enrollments. "No pass, no play" legislation (participation in after-school music events contingent upon passing grades in classes), meant to improve academic achievement, has hurt music ensembles and denied some at-risk students their main school interest and support group. When a student who feels isolated within the school environment is forced out of the only activities he or she finds meaningful, that student may choose to leave school.

Peer influence

Peer pressure can exert a powerful influence in the lives of youngsters. The Diamonds for Teens program is a peer assistance/leadership training program aimed at middle school and high school students in Carrollton, Texas. Diamonds for Teens addresses two mandated programs—at-risk students and gifted/talented students. Potential leaders called "diamonds in the rough" are identified and trained to work with at-risk peers. These "diamonds in the rough" come from all facets of the school environment and include cheerleaders, athletes, academically oriented students, students involved in the arts, students from special interest groups/clubs (such as student newspaper/publications, photography club, etc.), and recovering alcoholics and drug addicts. They are selected primarily by recommendations from administrators, teachers, counselors, and other students. "Diamonds" also undergo an interview and may participate in awareness training and role-playing exercises before being admitted to the Peer Assistance class (Crutsinger, 1991).

Comprehensive programs

Successful intervention programs are comprehensive in scope, addressing the home, the school system (grades K–12), and the community (Opuni, Tullis, & Sanchez, 1995). It is important to pay attention to at-risk students' transitions between schools. Community organizations and businesses can help relate academic skills to vocational skills by offering students out-of-school community service and paid work activities. Counseling services for at-risk youth must be ongoing, with attention to family interactions, health, and job placement.

The Oakland County Attendance and Dropout Task Force in Michigan was organized when principals asked for assistance in lowering the statewide dropout rate of 24%. The six guiding premises of the task force are:

1. Early identification and intervention are most important.
2. Schools cannot solve the dropout problem alone; it is a home, school, and community problem and must be resolved by everyone working together.
3. A variety of strategies will be needed; there is no single solution to these problems.
4. A strong attendance policy is needed; however, it is recognized that this is only one aspect of the dropout prevention program.
5. The Oakland County Task Force will serve as the catalyst in organizing local task forces in each of the 28 participating school districts.
6. The objectives of the Oakland County Task Force will be based on the needs of all 28 school districts; however, implementing specific programs will be the responsibility of the local school district. (Grossnickle, 1986, pp.16–17)

The Oakland County plan involves three phases:

■ *Phase I*—Establish a task force made up of 145 people from education, business, community agencies, recent high school graduates, parents, law enforcement, civic organizations, and the religious community.

- *Phase II*—Establish an advisory coalition of 14 people to exchange and share ideas, information, and resources and to develop a plan of action for local schools.
- *Phase III*—Organize a task force in each school district that is responsible for identifying resources within each community including funding sources, programs, and specialized personnel.

Another dropout prevention program at Addison Trail High School in Addison, Illinois (a suburb of Chicago), consists of three parts:

- *Part 1*—All freshmen are required to participate in the MOD (module of time) reading program instead of having a traditional unstructured study hall. Topics in the MOD program include study skills; reasons for staying in school; the value of grades, motivation, and self-esteem; how to handle peer pressure; choices for extracurricular activities; behavior guidelines; guidance services, and drug awareness. Freshmen are also required to participate in a developmental or corrective reading program staffed by a specialist who provides individual tutoring and computer-assisted instruction. "The key to the success of the MOD program is an adviser who takes a personal interest in each freshman" (Grossnickle, 1986, p. 18).
- *Part 2*—The Pupil Personnel Committee is made up of the school psychologist, social worker, assistant principal, guidance director, dean, and special education department chair. This committee reviews referrals from school staff and parents and recommends special programs for students identified as potential dropouts.
- *Part 3*—Students who are still unable to function successfully after having been provided with special services at their high schools have the option of attending Ombudsman Educational Services, Ltd. of Libertyville, Illinois. Illinois school districts pay about $2,200 for each student sent to Ombudsman. These fees are reimbursed by the state. Ombudsman uses diagnostic testing, prescriptions, treatment, and evaluation to develop an individualized program for each student. Appropriate goals are established, and a contract concerning the sending school,

Ombudsman staff, the student, and parents is drawn up. Students must achieve 90% mastery of the goals stated in that contract before new goals can be set. The program centers around the "intrinsic value of learning outcomes and career/life preparation." Four basic rules enforced at Ombudsman are: (1) the student must attend every day, (2) the student must make reasonable progress, (3) the student must never interfere with the learning of others, and (4) any student using drugs, alcohol, or tobacco will be suspended. The program has experienced great success: Ninety percent of Ombudsman students graduate from high school.

Summary

There is no easy solution to the problem of students at risk. "Quick fixes" may seem promising at first, but fail to produce lasting results. Programs such as ability tracking and "no pass, no play" rules tend to discourage students and frequently result in increased dropout rates. There are success stories, however, as evidenced by the model programs presented in this chapter. Although different, these successful approaches have several factors in common. Music educators can strive to promote these factors in their own programs:

- *Individualization.* Successful interventions are sensitive to the individual student, the school, and the community. Successful strategies reflect awareness of culture and gender.
- *High expectations.* Successful programs tend to be academically rigorous and demand excellence from all students.
- *Early intervention* The most effective strategies include early intervention. Head Start has proved to be an effective early-intervention strategy.
- *Parental involvement.* The home and the community are important considerations. The role of the parent is critical.
- *Motivation.* Successful programs include experiences that are motivating and invite active student participation in learning.
- *Peer influence.* Peer pressure is often a negative influence in the lives of at-risk students, but it can also be used as a

powerful tool for intervention. Peer assistance programs offer many benefits for both at-risk students and their peer tutors.

- *Comprehensiveness.* Successful programs are long term and address the "total student." It is important for students to see validity and consistency across the curriculum. The school day must be perceived as an integrated whole rather than as a series of unrelated (and unimportant) periods.

Chapter 4

The Role of Music and the Other Arts

The most effective at-risk programs are schoolwide. They address the entire school environment and involve everyone on the school staff. When at-risk students are identified, all the teachers and supporting staff must be informed. Working together as a team, faculty help students view the school day as a meaningful whole. Students then begin to recognize consistent relationships among people and activities, and the school day becomes more than just a fragmented procession of unrelated learning periods and seemingly uncaring adults.

Successful intervention programs pay special attention to the at-risk student during school transitions (the student's first year of school at a new campus, for example). In these instances, music educators can be of great assistance. Music classes are a perfect venue for building self-esteem and social skills. Prior to school transitions (from elementary school to middle school and from middle school to high school), music teachers at each school can collaborate in encouraging students to continue music participation. A student's fear of the unknown may be somewhat alleviated by meeting the new school's music teacher prior to the transition. Summer music programs at the upper-level school can ease students into the new environment. Receiving approval for their musical growth and importance to the ensemble can enhance their sense of belonging and self-esteem.

Hanna (1992) suggests that arts programs help children to understand their place in society and to become productive citizens. According to Godfrey (1992), children can relate to their own culture, the culture of their school, and the culture of others through the arts. "Art tracks civilization. That is its reality and its freedom" (p. 600).

Music study can improve students' critical thinking and reasoning skills (Hanna, 1992). It has been linked to improvements in spatial reasoning, which is the kind of reasoning required for mathematics, geometry, and engineering (Rauscher, 1994). Involvement in music activities offers experiences that are more compatible with the learning styles and emotional needs of at-risk students. For example, active participation in music and the arts builds self-esteem in students whose learning styles favor hands-on experiences. Furthermore, students who have difficulty in other subjects may have musical aptitudes and interests. For them, the study of music may make the difference between failure and success. Performing in a music ensemble can provide students with a socially acceptable form of emotional release that is necessary for their mental health. Successful ensemble participation emphasizes the importance of the individual to the group, thus helping at-risk students feel a sense of belonging.

Other subjects can be reinforced in music classes, making them more relevant to students' lives. Basic concepts can be taught through music activities or used as tools for learning musical concepts. In the first instance, asking young children to sing the alphabet to the tune of "Twinkle, Twinkle, Little Star" and teaching them to count by singing the tune "Six Little Ducks" are obvious examples. Examples of the second instance include learning fractions by playing and calculating the subdivisions in rhythms and meters, or exploring a social studies topic through the music of a particular historical period. School becomes more valuable to students when they see the relevance of other subjects to an area of personal interest, such as music.

Breaking the cycle of failure

A lack of success and feelings of alienation within the school environment may place a student at risk. A growing body of evidence suggests that these problems may be related to certain biases in traditional approaches to education.

Research in individual differences indicates that students require different educational settings and instructional approaches to achieve academic success (e.g., Coleman & Hardin, 1995; Gregorc, 1985; Hanson, 1990). The traditional classroom can become a very uncomfortable place for minority students and disadvantaged students—students whose cultural perspectives may be drastically different from those of their teachers (Garrett, 1995). Sights, sounds, and emotions explored through the arts may provide those students with a critical link between the sometimes alien world of the classroom and the "ways of knowing" that are more familiar to them (Hanson, Silver, & Strong, 1991).

In his Theory of Multiple Intelligences, Howard Gardner (1985) identified seven different competencies or "intelligences":

- *Verbal/linguistic intelligence*—relates to words and language
- *Logical/mathematical intelligence*—involves inductive and deductive thinking, numbers, and pattern recognition
- *Visual/spatial intelligence*—involves the ability to visualize an object and to create mental images and pictures
- *Body/kinesthetic intelligence*—relates to physical movement and the control of bodily motion
- *Musical/rhythmic intelligence*—involves the recognition of tonal patterns, including environmental sounds, and a sensitivity to rhythm and beats
- *Interpersonal intelligence*—involves person-to-person relationships and communication
- *Intrapersonal intelligence*—involves self-reflection, metacognition, and awareness of spirituality

Traditional instruction emphasizes the verbal/linguistic and logical/mathematical intelligences, but it has been suggested that students have different dominant intelligences (Gardner, 1985). Gardner points out the importance of teaching for all seven intelligences to enable students to attain optimum intellectual and emotional development. The need for instructional experiences that tap other competencies such as musical/rhythmic may be especially critical for disadvantaged learners (Lazear, 1991a).

Music and the arts can provide effective intervention for many of the problems associated with students at risk (Hanson, 1990; Marshall, 1978). Barry, Taylor, and Walls (1990) interviewed students identified as "at-risk" by their schools. Their arts teachers and school administrators were also interviewed. These interviews and on-site observations revealed that participation in fine arts courses gave these students opportunities for positive interactions with peers and adults, opportunities to experience pride in accomplishment, and a supportive and nurturing learning environment. Statements from administrators, teachers, and students confirmed that these arts courses were the only reasons many of these students remained in school.

Low self-concept is frequently associated with the at-risk phenomenon. Lacking confidence in their own abilities, students may choose to give up on school, the system, and themselves. Participation in the arts may help break this vicious cycle of failure by providing students opportunities to experience success. Interests and talents that might otherwise remain untapped can be awakened by arts experiences.

Minority students, who may feel out of place in the school environment, may deliberately choose academic failure as a way to assert their refusal to "buy into" the mainstream culture (Ogbu, 1992; Ogbu & Simons, 1994). Peer pressure can also be a powerful force against school success. "Of all the obstacles to success that inner-city black students face, the most surprising—and discouraging—may be those erected by their own peers ... Promising black students are ridiculed for speaking standard English, showing an interest in ballet or theater, having white friends, or joining activities other than sports" (Gregory, 1992, p. 44). Music and the arts can bridge cultural differences by helping students see the relevance of school to their own culture and to understand and appreciate the culture of others. "Not only will students see that people are different, but they will learn that there is a spirit represented in the arts that crosses human boundaries" (Taylor & Anderson, 1993, p. 5).

Integrating the curriculum

A number of successful school programs have included the arts as an integral part of the curriculum. The St. Augustine School (South Bronx, New York), the Robert E. Lee Elementary School (Columbia, Missouri), the Guggenheim School (Chicago), the KEY School (Indianapolis), Sanchez Elementary School (Austin, Texas), the Mead School (Byram, Connecticut), the Elm School (Milwaukee), the Comer Process

(Yale University), Central Park East (Harlem, New York), the Learning to Read through the Arts program (New York City), LEAP (New York City), and the Cleveland School System (Cleveland, Tennessee) have demonstrated that students from diverse backgrounds can achieve academic success in programs that emphasize creative arts experiences. These programs will be described in the next section.

Successful school programs

The St. Augustine School is a private elementary school (mostly black students) in South Bronx, New York. By 1984, the dropout problem was so severe that the student body had been reduced from 500 to 118 students. In that year, the arts school across the street (directed by Tom Pilecki) and its curriculum were integrated into the St. Augustine School. The school and its children underwent a remarkable transformation.

Pilecki, the principal of St. Augustine Elementary School, describes the approach he used with students and parents:

> My first job was to empower and instruct those who were the closest—the children and the parents. We started an intense two months of meetings and information sessions. And basically I just told them very simply what we proposed to do, and that was to enhance what those kids already had with an arts program. We did something that was natural. This is what the children need. Why? Because we are dealing with children who are unhappy, very unhappy in these situations. These are single-parent families, and most parents are nowhere around. So the natural alternative is to find things that are going to interest these children. It is natural. This is not something spectacularly special. We are talking about things that should be happening in our children's lives. So what we did was simply look at what our children needed. That was in the spring of '84. In the fall of '85, we opened St. Augustine School of the Arts. (Pilecki, 1989, p. 38)

More than 90% of St. Augustine's students now read at grade level (only three New York grade schools can claim that distinction), and the cost per pupil is unusually low: only $3000 annually per student (compared to a New York City average of almost $8,000).

The Robert E. Lee Elementary School in Columbia, Missouri, developed an arts-centered curriculum. This program has four components: (1) a language arts program emphasizing creative writing and literature, (2) an expanded art and music program that is integrated into other subject areas, (3) implementation of the Missouri Council of Arts Artist-In-Residence Program, and (4) an extended-day arts enrichment program. The school's philosophy emphasizes the arts throughout the curriculum:

> We value the uniqueness, language, culture, and experiences
> each child brings to the learning environment. The arts, in
> addition to being disciplines themselves, are the most natural
> way to explore, experience and express learning in other areas.
> (Schlimme, 1990, p. 4)

The Guggenheim School implemented accelerated learning techniques and an integrated curriculum based on Howard Gardner's Multiple Intelligence Theory (1985). In one year, this inner-city Chicago school went from last place (out of the 17 school districts) to first place in academic achievement (Lazear, 1991b). Teachers participated in a series of workshops in instructional methods for integrating the arts. They had instruction in memory techniques, relaxation strategies, and social and personal skills. Subsequent workshops provided teachers with training in drama and visual arts. Both teacher and student attendance increased after the program was implemented. Lazear reports that teacher sick-leave days were reduced by 96% and that average daily student attendance rose to 94%. He also reported that 83% of the students achieved reading and mathematics scores that were equal to or above the national norms for reading and math.

The KEY School in Indianapolis is another example of a program based on Gardner's theory of multiple intelligences (Lazear, 1991b). Formed by teachers who had become disenchanted with traditional schools, the KEY School allows each student to explore and develop a variety of competencies. Students with different abilities and backgrounds are admitted to the school by lottery. Instruction in music and the arts is not looked upon as a frill or as an extracurricular activity. Starting in kindergarten, the arts are an integral part of the curriculum for every student. Creative dramatics, dance, visual arts, and music are offered as separate subjects and are integrated throughout the curriculum to involve students in learning. Students flourish in this environment. Recent Indiana State Educational Proficiency test scores indicated achievement at or above grade level for 98% of the students in the KEY School (MacRae-Campbell, 1991a).

Sometimes music educators try to build their students' self-esteem through the selection of songs with positive lyrics.

Barb Stevanson at Sanchez Elementary School (preK–6, year-round attendance) in Austin, Texas, organized a music and art program funded by the local school district that involved first, second, fifth, and sixth graders. Students performed songs and created visual art to learn about building positive self-esteem for themselves and for others. Sanchez Elementary School is 98% Hispanic. At Sanchez, 25–30% of the children speak only Spanish, 25–30% speak only English, and the remainder are bilingual. Most of the children (80–85%) receive free or reduced-price lunches.

The Mead School in Greenwich, Connecticut, serves a diverse student population. Each student at this elementary school spends approximately half the school day studying basic skills through integrated activities that involve painting, weaving, music, and movement. The second half of the day is used for specialized arts instruction (Lazear, 1991b). Students' average Stanford Achievement Test (SAT) scores are equal to or above their grade level in every subject. Students with below-average SATs in their first three years at the school experienced large gains in achievement by their fifth and sixth year (Oddleifson, 1992). Teachers at the Mead School attribute student success to the arts-enriched learning environment.

The Elm Creative Arts School in Milwaukee, Wisconsin, is an example of another elementary school that has integrated the arts throughout the curriculum. The arts are used in three ways at Elm: (1) as an integral part of every subject in every classroom, (2) as separate classes, and (3) as a way to show interrelationships among the different arts (e.g., students learn that rhythm is important in both music and dance and that color is important in painting and writing). At Elm, teachers integrate the arts to enhance student understanding whenever possible. All students are enrolled in specialized arts instruction. The arts classes are not considered extracurricular; rather, they are an important part of the school day. The Elm School is considered one of the best elementary schools in the country and has consistently ranked number one academically in the Milwaukee School District (Oddleifson, 1992).

The Comer Process was developed for disadvantaged minority elementary students by James Comer (1984) at the Yale University Child Study Center. It includes four components: (1) a school advisory council consisting of the principal and representatives of teachers, teacher aides, and parents; (2) a mental health team comprised of a school psychologist and support personnel; (3) a parent participation program; and (4) a flexible academic program that integrates the teaching of basic social skills with the arts. This is one of the few programs achieving full parental participation. Parents serve on the school advisory council, work as paid part-time aides, volunteer at the school, and receive counseling from the mental health team.

Academic achievement and student attendance increased at the inner-city elementary schools where the Comer Process was implemented. Comer also pointed out that behavior problems decreased, saying that: "the strength of this project is its focus on the entire school rather than on any one particular aspect, and its attention to institutional change rather than on any individual change" (Dryfoos, 1990, p. 205).

Central Park East, a school for seventh through twelfth graders in East Harlem, is based on the theories of Ted Sizer and the Coalition of Essential Schools (Sizer, 1984). The coalition emphasizes in-depth learning as opposed to fragmented curricula. The intense seven- through tenth-grade classical curriculum at Central Park East includes arts electives (scheduled before 9:00 A.M. or between 3:00 and 5:00 P.M. The eleventh- and twelfth-grade curricula are individualized and may include out-of-school experiences. All students work two hours per week in school or community service. Teachers meet with advisory groups of 15 students (Dryfoos, 1990) for daily counseling sessions.

The Learning to Read through the Arts (LRTA) program was developed in a New York City elementary school. It has improved student motivation and K–12 test scores with its music- and arts-centered curriculum. The curriculum is so effective that it "greatly reduces the need for expensive special education pullouts" (Shuler, 1991, p. 27). In response to this success, many school systems throughout the United States are adopting LRTA.

LEAP (Learning through an Expanded Arts Program) is a nonprofit education organization in New York City. LEAP's goal is to improve the quality of education in the city's five boroughs. For 14 years, it has served more than 400,000 students. LEAP has enlisted the aid of more than 85 consultants (including many art and music professionals) to work with students in grades K–8 and to train teachers to integrate the arts in the academic curriculum. Consultants team teach with classroom teachers, who eventually continue projects on their own. LEAP projects are diverse, including architecture, archaeology, robotics, opera composing, videotaping, and African storytelling. Regardless of the project, the central focus is on enhancing students' basic skills:

The arts-oriented approach to learning developed by LEAP adheres to the conditions necessary for learning. First, the materials and projects are intrinsically interesting to students and make learning an exciting experience. Second, the sense of accomplishment that comes from the completion of a creative task helps students develop self-confidence and self-esteem. When they are part of a LEAP project, academic assignments no longer hold the threat of failure and shame; instead, they represent opportunities for personal expression and success. (Dean & Gross, 1992, p. 614)

Arts education is an integral part of the core curriculum in the Cleveland, Tennessee, School System. An arts specialist teams up with classroom teachers to provide arts instruction for students. The specialist comes into the classroom for one hour every other week to teach an integrated lesson with an emphasis on arts experiences. The classroom teacher observes and assists. The following week, the classroom teacher leads students in an arts-related writing activity based on the specialist's lesson. Parents, teachers, and students are enthusiastic about the project. Teachers report that:

Student interest and motivation have also gone up, particularly among at-risk students. Cleveland students have shown across-the-board improvement in writing and cognitive skills. They've developed an interest in and knowledge of the arts that they would never have gained without this program. And they believe their ideas and experiences are valued. (Mernit, 1992, p. 46)

Despite financial constraints and a lack of arts resources, the Cleveland School System has developed an outstanding arts-in-the-curriculum program, demonstrating that "an exemplary arts program doesn't require big spending, just big ideas" (Mernit, 1992, p. 46).

"Sing, Spell, Read, and Write" (SSRW) is a language program for grades K–3 consisting of charts, books, letter and word cards, tests, and audio tapes of songs. The songs teach phonics through sounds of letters and letter combinations. SSRW was developed in 1984 and was implemented in 11 Memphis City Schools during the 1991–92 school year. A recent research study of the effectiveness of the SSRW program indicated that the program was beneficial, giving children a good foundation for reading and language arts. Because of the observed educational benefits, particularly for low-achieving kindergarten students, researchers recommended SSRW for schools having high numbers of at-risk students.

The researchers also observed that "teacher confidence in and enthusiasm toward SSRW is a definite positive factor, as was evident in teacher feedback" and "in addition to teacher enthusiasm toward SSRW, students and parents appear to like the program" (Bond, Smith, Ross, Nunnery, & Goldstein, 1992, p. 4).

Magnet schools

Magnet schools have specific curricula and attract talented students from broad geographical areas. Arts magnet schools, for example, offer special training in visual arts, music, dance, and drama; some of them also offer complete college preparatory studies in the high school grades. Grade levels range from K–12 (occasionally K–14), and many schools are members of a common professional organization—the International Network of Performing and Visual Arts Schools. Gordon (1993) surveyed 44 magnet schools belonging to this organization and found that most of the schools served grades 9–12 and ranged in size from 105 to 804 students with music enrollment ranges from 2 to 300. Although some of the schools could not recruit outside their school districts, 50% could recruit statewide. Gordon found that the "missions of arts schools were divided evenly among preprofessional training institutions, schools with a college preparatory emphasis, and schools seeking to provide the best general education possible" (p. viii). Arts magnet schools may be good models for studying the effects of the arts upon at-risk children. Descriptions of four different schools are given in the following section.

The Ashley River Creative Arts Magnet School (Charleston County, South Carolina) serves a diverse student population of 475 pupils (K–5), which are selected by lottery. (There is a waiting list of about 1200 children, with some parents submitting applications before the child is born.) In addition to regular state and local academic requirements, students receive creative arts instruction for an average of one hour a day, including music, art, drama/creative writing, dance/gymnastics, Suzuki strings, and Spanish. The arts are also integrated with other subjects in the curriculum. Although the school is located in what has been called a "problem area," students at Ashley River consistently outperform other students in their county and state on standardized achievement tests. Daily student attendance rates average 97%, and parent attendance at PTA meetings is always 100% ("You Gotta Have Art," 1991). All this is accomplished without lengthening the school day and only spending about $15.00 more per pupil than other elementary schools in the district.

Although not strictly designed for at-risk students, the Fillmore Arts Center in Washington, D.C., is an unusual example of a magnet school that serves all 900 students in a cluster of small schools (five schools, grades K–8). The five schools are located within a three-mile radius of Fillmore, and students are bused to Fillmore for a half day every week. They participate in dance, drama, music, visual arts, creative writing, and physical education. Interschool cooperation is important. Fillmore's artist/teachers (all are part-time staff) visit the other five schools in the cluster to become acquainted with the teachers and the schools. Likewise, teachers from the cluster regularly sit in on classes at Fillmore to become familiar with the arts curriculum. Evaluation of student progress, teachers, and programs is emphasized at Fillmore. In this setting, the teachers feel that their school "not only provides students with arts literacy but also with opportunities to develop personal frames of reference to interpret other subjects, to test principles, and to evaluate life experiences" (Mitchell, Lesser, & Stroblas, 1988, p. 22).

The Region 7 Middle School, a successful Detroit magnet school, stresses student self-direction and responsibility through active student involvement and strict behavioral standards. Class schedules and teacher teams change every nine weeks so that students may choose from more than 100 courses. Students have independent study time during the day and participate in ungraded minicourses such as chess, art, African folk tales, and other topics suggested by students. Region 7 involves students and parents in school policy decisions. Average daily attendance at Region 7 is much higher than at other schools in the district. Students' reading scores have also improved (Dryfoos, 1990).

The Carver Creative and Performing Arts Center (CCPAC), another magnet school, is part of the Montgomery, Alabama, public school system. Students in grades 10–12 who live in the school district and want to attend the center must audition for it, since enrollment is limited (the 1993 enrollment was 345 students). Sixteen arts areas are offered, including dance, creative writing, mass media, visual arts, and a variety of music and drama offerings. Students may choose to combine their arts diploma program with a college preparatory curriculum or just to concentrate in the arts diploma program. Once admitted, all students who ask for scholarships receive them. CCPAC boasts that 49% of their graduating seniors received scholarships for further study at other institutions. Students must maintain a C grade point average to remain in the program, but CCPAC will accept at-risk students with poor grades or learning disorders—particularly when the right mixture of enthusiasm and (perhaps) hidden talent is observed. Cheryl Carter, the director, cites the example of a learning disabled young man who was allowed to enter the visual arts program with desire as his only viable credential. By his third year, he had become an accomplished artist and even succeeded in the piano program. The combination of this young man's enthusiasm and his growing self-esteem in the arts "really changed his self-concept. He emerged as a leader" (Bartocci, 1992, p. 34).

Arts magnet schools continue to be popular (see, for example, stories about magnet schools in "You Gotta Have Art," *USA Today,* April 17, 1991), and it is important that more research be directed toward understanding their effect on the world of art, student motivation, at-risk students, and learning in general. Gordon (1993) understood the need for this kind of research and developed a follow-up questionnaire for graduates of arts magnet schools. Perhaps this questionnaire will be used by some magnet schools to assess their alumni.

School/community partnerships

There is an increasing body of literature indicating that the arts provide effective intervention for many of the problems associated with disadvantaged and at-risk students. The College of Education (program in music education) at Auburn University and the Auburn University Cooperative Extension Service initiated a project addressing the problem of youth at risk. This approach advocates:

> the application of education and experience in the arts within a nurturing environment through a cooperative and collaborative program between schools and communities. The program model is based on the concept that a child, in order to receive adequate nurturing toward the end of leading a successful life, must receive help, encouragement, and support from three societal anchors—parents, schools, and community. The concept further acknowledges that a child has a good chance of

success when support is obtained from at least two of the three anchors. However, at-risk youth are often observed to receive little or no support from any of these three vitalities. (Johnson & Barry, 1993, p. 63–70)

The arts and youth at-risk project in Alabama was originally conceived by music educators, but it evolved into a collaboration between music educators and the Alabama Cooperative Extension Service. This alliance was formed because both the music educators and the extension service personnel were concerned with the national agenda of youth at-risk. The music educator's interest in using community resources more effectively to provide fine arts programs for youngsters and the extension service personnel's interest in increasing their community-based programs in the schools (such as 4-H) resulted in the pooling of resources and expertise to develop the community/arts plan. A series of sessions produced an outline for a special conference on the arts and at-risk students that would bring together personnel from education, extension services, business, and other community representatives. The music educators contacted school personnel in target counties. Extension personnel worked through county agents to contact community representatives from business, juvenile courts, police agencies, social service providers, housing project offices, and arts associations. They also reinforced the contacts already made by the music educators. School and community teams were mobilized in advance of the conference and preliminary meetings were held.

The conference was titled "The At-Risk Child and the Arts: A School and Community Partnership." The representative of a prominent local corporation presented an address on "The State and Community: The Economics of Educating At-Risk Children," followed by responses from an educator and an extension community development specialist. Other sessions featured speakers from the urban and rural public school systems, Alabama State Department of Education personnel, a juvenile court judge, a state senator, a public school music educator, and an art educator. These sessions provided appropriate background for the conference, but most participants agreed that the most valuable components of the conference were the Team Process Times. At these sessions, the participants came together to discuss options and strategies unique to the needs and resources within their particular communities. A Team Process Kit containing detailed step-by-step instructions for developing school and community partnerships was mailed to each team leader prior to the conference. This kit was the foundation for the interaction and exchange of ideas that occurred during the Team Process Time. Many participants commented that they were surprised to learn that educators, extension personnel, business leaders, and other community leaders shared many common interests and concerns regarding the arts and at-risk students.

On an evaluation form, 83% of the participants stated that the subject of the conference was "very relevant" to education problems in their county, 77% were "very interested" in using the arts in working with the problems of at-risk children in their county, 93% said that a partnership between the community and schools in their county would be "very strong" (50%) or "possible" (43%), and 90% were interested in a conference follow-up. This conference demonstrated that participating community and business leaders were aware of the potential benefits of arts experiences for at-risk students and were interested in forming supportive partnerships with arts educators.

The T-LC Mentors Program in Ann Arbor, Michigan, spans the generation gap to provide support for at-risk students. Senior citizen volunteers serve as mentors for junior high school students. The volunteers meet with their assigned youngster at least once a week to work on projects that can include the arts (Sipe, Grossman, & Milliner, 1988). Interviews with both seniors and teens indicated much satisfaction with the project. Students enjoyed working with the senior citizens because they were not "professional or police." Seniors enjoyed having one-on-one interactions with the young people, and they enjoyed the opportunities to be creative (Dryfoos, 1990, p. 214).

Music teachers should not overlook potential collaborations with their colleagues in related arts and also in other disciplines. Ways of integrating music into the visual arts, for example, are well known to most music teachers, but using music in language, history, and science contexts perhaps presents greater challenges. For a variety of reasons, some music teachers may not wish to experiment with adding music to nonarts areas, but cannot ignore the fact that music can enhance the effectiveness of programs for at-risk students. In a survey of innovative at-risk/dropout programs throughout Florida, Taylor and Davis (1996) found that of the 54 programs identified in this project, 40 involve arts as only part of the program (the remaining 14 are total arts programs). Most of these program directors believe that music and the other arts are important elements in their curricula, and many had

asked music teachers and other musicians to actively participate in the program or to provide advice about the kinds of
music to be used and ways to use it. Interestingly, fewer than
half (16) of these 40 programs are sponsored by individual
schools or by school districts. The remaining 24 are sponsored
by other organizations: Florida's Juvenile Justice Department,
departments of parks and recreation (city and county), cultural
units supported by state, federal, and/or private grants (muse-
ums, orchestras, dance and theater companies, etc.), hospitals
and special centers (that deal with emotional and behavioral
health problems), and special programs funded by the city or
county. This survey provides strong evidence that music teachers can, and should, cooperate with other teachers in adding
music to curriculum-integrated at-risk programs—especially
since all respondents to the survey rated their programs quite
highly in improving their students' social skills, academic
skills, and general behavior.

School/university partnerships

A partnership began as an informal agreement between
Lee County (a rural Alabama school system) and the Auburn
University College of Education. In this reciprocal arrangement, the county school students benefited from having arts
instruction and the university students benefited from having
field experiences. This arrangement served as the beginning
for what evolved into a more focused effort to bring the arts
into the Lee County Schools. Continued interaction between
the school system and the university over a two-year period
fostered the development of mutual respect and trust between
key personnel, an essential element of successful school/uni-
versity partnerships. As support for the arts increased within
the school system, a team of interested Lee County teachers
and administrators and an Auburn University music education
professor was assembled.

The team provided the focus and leadership needed to
move forward. A Special Projects Grant from the Alabama
State Council on the Arts funded a countywide needs assessment. Results of the assessment pointed out the importance of
increasing opportunities for arts experiences within the county
schools. Model programs were identified through a literature
review, and a program founded upon Discipline-Based Arts
Education in Cleveland, Tennessee, was selected as an appro-

priate model for the Lee County Schools. Grant funds were used to send a team of five Lee County teachers and the music education professor to visit schools in Cleveland in the spring of 1995.

The Cleveland trip was both informative and inspirational for team members. Being able to see the way that the arts can stimulate thinking and motivate students (particularly at-risk students) provided new impetus for the Lee County effort. Two Lee County teachers returned to Cleveland in the summer of 1995 to receive special training in Discipline-Based Arts Education. These two teachers served as peer trainers throughout the following school year, providing in-service training for peers. The school system continues to seek ways to provide arts experiences for all students, including hiring additional arts specialists, providing arts in-service for teachers, and submitting applications for additional grant funding (Barry, 1995).

Arts advocacy groups

The value of the arts in education is recognized and supported by a number of alliances and coalitions across the nation. The Center for the Arts in the Basic Curriculum (CABC) is an arts advocacy group that actively campaigns for the inclusion of the arts as an integral part of the public school curriculum. CABC was founded by the trustees and supporters of the South Shore Conservatory in Hingham and Duxbury, Massachusetts. It was founded on the premise that:

> The arts should be the very basis of education ... CABC believes that the arts should play a primary role in the restructuring of American education, which includes new approaches to curriculum and teaching.
> An examination of those schools that have made the arts the basis of education indicates several things in common: they raise academic test scores, often dramatically; they enhance pupils' self-esteem, teacher relations and parental involvement; they lower disciplinary actions and suspension/dropout rates; they maintain high daily attendance, they re-energize teachers and awaken their latent creative capabilities. Above all, they increase the quality of personal performance at all behavioral levels—and they foster respect among individual students. (Oddleifson, 1991, p. 2)

Special projects

Even when the arts are not fully integrated into the school curriculum, their presence in school-based at-risk intervention programs enhances the success of the programs through increased self-esteem and academic achievement.

Project ARISE (Arts Restoring and Increasing Self-Esteem) was a pilot summer program providing arts enrichment activities for 42 Alabama children (ages 5–13) enrolled in a special day care facility for low-income minority families. A majority of these children were classified as "at-risk" due to factors including: single-parent household, child of teenage mother, one or both parents dropped out of school, low socioeconomic status, victim of neglect, or victim of abuse. The Piers-Harris Children's Self-Concept Scale was administered before and after participation in 24 hours of arts activities. Additional data were obtained through focused observations and individual interviews with participants. Comparison of pretest and posttest Piers-Harris scores indicated significant improvement for total self-concept and for four attitudinal cluster scores: school status; physical appearance; and attributes, anxiety, and happiness. The frequency and duration of constructive interaction with peers and adults increased. The effect that creative arts experiences had upon these students was expressed by the girl who explained that the project was helpful to her "because now I like myself" (Barry, 1992, p. 4).

The Assured Readiness for Learning program in New York City uses music, art, and physical education "to enhance the child's mental and physical development" (Shuler, 1991, p. 26). Studies indicate that this arts-rich curriculum has reduced student failures and has increased language-arts achievement.

The RITA (Reading Improvement through Art) program at John F. Kennedy High School in New York City was designed for tenth graders with low reading scores. The written work for the course was based on daily arts experiences with students who maintained two portfolios, one containing their visual designs and one containing their written work. For every six months in the program, students gained one year in reading achievement as measured by standardized test scores. Test scores and student records indicate that students' sequential and verbal abilities were strengthened (photocopied pamphlet provided by the Center for Arts in the Basic Curriculum).

Studying the Environment through the Arts is a multidisciplinary approach to environmental education for high-risk high school students in Leon County, Florida. High school music specialists, classroom teachers, county administrators, museum and zoo personnel, media specialists, and university dance and composition faculty collaborate to provide students with integrated learning experiences in science, geography, history, critical thinking, problem solving, and evaluation skills. This project culminates with a "multisite and multimovement work called Earthworks" (Hughes, 1992, p. 20).

Another innovative program is a special adaptation of the Florida Department of Education's Introduction to Music Performance in Leon County, Florida. Funded through a grant from the Florida Fine Arts Council, this general music course provides a mainstreamed high school general music class with a variety of music experiences. Designed for students of diverse abilities and motivation, the course seeks to involve students with hands-on experiences. A special feature of the course includes visits from professional, amateur, and student musicians representing a wide range of musical styles (Hughes, 1992).

The ESOL/Bilingual Counseling Program in the Montgomery (Alabama) County Public Schools provides counseling services for students from 112 countries in grades K–12. A team of nine bilingual counselors, including one trained art therapist, uses artwork as a tool for working with youth at risk and with cross-cultural populations. "Art transcends language barriers because it is a nonverbal medium and the symbols are universal. Therefore, the students can express themselves freely" (Dapena, Gatti, & Nadal, 1991, p. 113). Many of the students in this program have experienced traumatic events such as sexual abuse, poverty, famine, and war. "Verbal expression of these feelings can often be difficult due to the nature of the traumatic event or the limited proficiency in English. Through the artwork, a counselor is able to ascertain a wealth of information about the child" (p. 113). The arts component of this counseling program successfully provided the students with opportunities to share feelings in a nonverbal manner, promoted positive self-esteem by creating artworks, and established a "working alliance" by cultivating a trusting relationship with the counselor through nonverbal communication.

Hadley and Hadley (1991) have developed a program to motivate and teach at-risk students. This program focuses on using music to motivate students to develop skills in language arts, mathematics, and social studies. Young children participate in musical activities to develop skills in the language arts. These activities include forming letters with their bodies to music, and describing and identifying color pictures when color words are used in songs. Music is also used to develop critical-thinking skills and to reinforce the student's knowledge of mathematical concepts. The authors explain:

> Students have always responded to music because they can participate physically and socially. Musical experiences that encourage students to become active and creative provide a greater stimulus for developing critical-thinking skills ...
> Music is called the universal language because man's experiences and emotions are expressed through the same musical notations. Joy, sorrows, love of country, loneliness, and humor are expressed through music ... Reading and music can serve to enhance the critical-thinking skills of students in all content areas including language arts, mathematics, art, and social studies. (pp. 54–55)

Tapping into student creativity

Case studies lend insight into some of the circumstances that place students at risk. Many of these studies illustrate the importance of hands-on, creative activities for motivating at-risk students. When a young man on death row was asked to describe a school "that could help a person like him" he talked about a program where "after lunch, we would do something creative with our hands" (Strother, 1991, p. 30).

Published case studies specifically related to arts experiences and at-risk students are rare, but those that are available offer powerful evidence for the value of music and the arts as catalysts for increased self-esteem, enhanced motivation, and academic improvement. One story describes a high school student whose involvement and success in an electronic music course led to increased confidence and academic achievement. The student explained his success in this way:

> It [the electronic music course] challenged me to learn to think. It gave me an opportunity to experiment with great equipment. It helped me to be creative and in a style I enjoyed. It gave me the confidence and self-esteem I lacked. It changed my life. (Modugno, 1991, p. 54)

Another case chronicles the way involvement in a musical program brought about dramatic changes in the life of an academically and emotionally troubled fifth grader. His music teacher described the way this child's participation in music and dramatics fostered a sense of self-worth and belonging in the school environment:

> I marveled at how profoundly a student's sense of worth can be shaped by the opportunity to make a meaningful contribution—even as the student struggles with all the same inadequacies that were once such convincing evidence of his or her failure. It seems that by respectfully accepting the gifts that students offer, we allow them to accept the help they need with dignity. (Niebur, 1992, p. 9)

In other case studies, students have benefited when music educators have composed songs for them. Jim Marshall began writing songs that he accompanied on his electronic keyboard to help Henderson Middle School (El Paso, Texas) students learn English vocabulary. His idea was successful, so he began a performing group, "The Lamplighters." This group meets after school to rehearse songs Marshall has written to increase self-esteem and to encourage youngsters to stay away from drugs. They have performed at retirement homes and conventions (Lynn, 1992).

Ed Doran teaches music at Colonial Hills Elementary School in San Antonio, Texas. He decided that his students needed to understand that making a wrong choice in behavior does not make one a "bad person," but making the right choices leads to happier lives. He writes musicals to teach the participants self-esteem. The songs and dances combine Orff instruments and MIDI accompaniments with lyrics such as "Don't live your life with low expectations, you have the know-how. Be a sensation" (Doran, 1992).

In another case study, Patricia Green and Norris Berry (1992) in Washington, D. C., composed songs in a contemporary style with positive messages that were relevant to their students' lives. Green and Berry (1992) found that their students responded favorably to the idea that the songs were written especially for them. The students also felt special because they knew the composers personally. This personal relationship with artists encouraged them to participate in learning.

Survey of state music consultants and music teachers

Although some programs that deal with music and at-risk students have been well-documented and publicized, others have not received much attention—either because they are in the beginning stages or because access to documentation is limited. In an attempt to learn more about these lesser-known programs, the authors of this book contacted the state music consultants—or fine arts consultants, if the state did not have a separate music consultant—in each of the 50 states. Twenty-six college music education faculty across the country also were contacted. The latter were selected on the basis of their knowledge of music education in the public and private school sectors. The state consultants and college faculty were asked to submit descriptions of unpublished, grassroots music-related at-risk projects within their geographical areas.

Thirteen state music consultants (from Alabama, Florida, Georgia, Illinois, Indiana, Louisiana, Mississippi, New York, Pennsylvania, South Carolina, Utah, Washington, and Wisconsin) and 12 of the college faculty responded to the survey (Taylor, 1993). Several programs were described, and those individuals responsible for these programs were contacted and asked to provide descriptions of their projects.

There are two similar projects in Columbia, South Carolina, and Tallahassee, Florida, that involve the MIE (Music in Education) MIDI keyboard laboratory developed by Yamaha Corporation. The MIE system is designed to train young students in basic musicianship, music appreciation, and keyboard skills. In Columbia, the laboratory is part of the curriculum for the Cities in Schools program, an alternative school, and is sponsored jointly by Yamaha, the local business community, and the School of Music at the University of South Carolina (C. A. Elliott, personal communication, Sept. 12, 1993). In Tallahassee, Yamaha is collaborating with the School of Music at Florida State University. MIE systems have been placed at three Tallahassee elementary schools: Riley, Pineview, and Bond. To date, these systems have been used extensively with several classes, including at-risk students. Evaluations of the Columbia and Tallahassee programs are underway. Included are measures of self-esteem, academic improvement, attendance, tardy records, and other factors (C. K. Madsen, personal communication, Sept. 12, 1993).

Melinda Biggars, a classroom music teacher (grades 1–6) in Riverview, Florida, reported that music recently has been "integrated into the total literacy curriculum [at her elementary school] and will be focusing on cooperative learning activities to better develop social skills as well as language skills of migrant students." She states that "the three-year goal is to raise test scores of the Stanford Achievement Test and make the children at Wimauma Elementary comparable with other children of more affluent schools in Hillsborough County." Melinda believes that participation in a variety of music activities (strings, Orff, recorders, folk dancing, chorus, etc.) in the context of the rest of the curriculum "reinforces reading skills, expression, social skills, and critical-thinking skills" (M. Biggars, personal communication, Aug. 20, 1993).

The arts in Hillsborough County, Florida, have also been strongly supported through the Hillsborough County Fine Arts Education Consortium. Under the aegis of the Minority Education Enhancement program, the Consortium sponsors a K–6 intervention program (The Rising Star Program: Success through the Arts) that is centered around the fine arts. The program is designed for both talented and at-risk minority students. They participate in "programmed arts activities which seek to excite, motivate, and enhance the appreciation of, and learning about, the fine arts" (P. J. Trice, personal communication, Aug. 25, 1993). The instructors are volunteers, and the center is located at West Tampa Elementary School. Activities consist of "standard classroom arts, performances by visiting artists and teachers, audiovisual presentations, creative projects, and small-group activities." Tutors are provided for "educational deficiencies which may exist within a given student." The Consortium believes that the fine arts can serve as a catalyst for learning productivity, socialization, self-confidence, and understanding the value of education through the "excitement and personal involvement that generally encompasses fine arts activities."

The SIMARS (Summer Instrumental Music for At-Risk Students) project in Topeka, Kansas, offers a four-week string and band program for at-risk students in the fourth through eighth grades. Larita Owens explains that "students in lower socioeconomic levels are invited to attend [the program] at no cost," and that "it keeps them playing their instruments four more weeks in the summer." The ensembles meet five days a week. Larita states that as a result of this extended learning, their self-esteem is boosted, especially when the students perform for their parents on the last day. Her comment about working with the students is heart-warming, and the last sentence should be noted by all educators:

> I love to work with them because it doesn't seem to take much to boost their self-confidence, once they see what they can do. I always remind them after each small success that they can be this successful in everything they do—it just takes a little work. Then we talk about everything they had to know to make

that "success" possible. (L. Owens, personal communication, Sept. 15, 1993)

Joyce Forest, a music teacher at Ortega Elementary School in Austin, Texas, describes a sizable grant awarded to her school for the purpose of developing and implementing a comprehensive program for at-risk students. Her narrative is reproduced in toto here.

April, 1991, marked the beginning of educational reform for Ortega Elementary in Austin, Texas. Designated a Next-Century School by the R. J. R. Nabisco Foundation, Ortega was awarded a three-year grant of $741,000 to restructure education for their at-risk students. The restructuring plan, called "Labs to Enrich and Accelerate Learning" (LEAL) was designed by the school's music teacher and librarian. It features an extended school day; a heavy concentration in the arts; and laboratories in science, math, computer, literature, music, photography, gymnastics, and Mexican folklorico dancing. A six-week accelerated summer school, featuring weekly field trips, is also included. Because of the grant funding, Ortega is the only school in Austin where all students are taught by specialists in music, art, physical education, science, literature, and math.

Ortega is located in an area of intense drug and gang activity. The ethnic mix is 70% Hispanic and 30% Black. Over 90% of the students are on free or reduced-price lunch. Although 46% of our children are classified as at risk by federal government specifications, the Ortega staff considers 100% of our students at risk!

Music at Ortega is experiential, and a key goal of LEAL is to increase each child's experiences and self-esteem. Young children explore many ways in which they can produce music. Early childhood learning centers are a key ingredient to classroom music for prekindergarten through grade two. During second and third grades, singing and music-reading skills are emphasized. Recorders and keyboards are introduced at the fourth-grade level, and our primary emphasis is participation in a music memory contest. Electronic music is fascinating to the fifth-grade students. The keyboard lab, interactive MIDI software for both Macintosh and IBM computers, drum machine, and synthesizer keep all learners engaged. Students work in cooperative learning groups and rotate through six stations in six class periods. Each group shares its music at the end of the class.

Fourteen talented third- through fifth-grade students are chosen to participate in the after-school keyboard lab (at no cost to the students). This year (the second year of the project), there are six second-year students and eight beginners. The students also play in ensemble, using a variety of instruments.

These ensembles encourage the students, because together they create music they would otherwise be unable to master at this early stage of their career.

In the second year of the LEAL project, 71% percent of Ortega third graders passed all three sections of the state-mandated achievement test (the state average was only 60%). Of the 66 elementary schools in Austin, Ortega ranked 16th in percentage of third graders passing all three sections. Incidentally, this year all fourth graders (except one) scored at or above the state average on this test. Currently, Ortega's average attendance rate is 98%.

Musically, the children are demonstrating more understanding of skills. 1993 is the fourth year younger children have experienced music centers. The opportunity to experience music and experiment with many instruments and sounds is meeting a need for these at-risk students. Ortega students are demonstrating rhythmic reading and pitch accuracy at earlier ages. There are fewer uncertain singers in the upper grades. Perhaps most importantly, Ortega students are having fun as they become better musicians. They are very proud of their musical abilities and enjoy sharing the music they are producing. Furthermore, the parents are excited about the opportunity their children have to play recorders and keyboard—and they attend performances.

We firmly believe that enriching activities—art, music, movement, dancing—are vital to the development of the whole child. The enrichment component of LEAL has a primary goal of increasing the student's self-esteem. We see strong indications that our "arts intensive" program is successful. Academically, there is documented proof. After the first complete year of our project, teachers noticed a difference in the attitudes of the 100 students who also attended summer school. They have become the leaders of their classes and they seem to be more responsive to motivational tactics. They have "bought into" their own education. Our faculty teach as though all children can learn. Only recently have our students and parents joined our cause. (J. Forest, personal communication, Sept. 15, 1993)

The music teachers and state consultants also were asked to cite reasons why they believe music experiences can contribute to helping at-risk students. These reasons are as follows:

- Music requires teamwork and thus helps to build social skills.
- The music environment is nonthreatening and allows students to improve naturally at their own rate and within their own limits.
- Everyone needs a creative outlet, and music provides the opportunity.

- Music accommodates a variety of learning types—the student becomes involved with the visual, aural, and kinesthetic modalities.
- Music reinforces reading and critical-thinking skills.

Furthermore, some very specific suggestions were made for teachers of nonarts classes. Certainly, these suggestions are just a few of the many possibilities. Nonarts classes could:

- Integrate rhythmic and melodic elements in their classes, thus resulting in more attentive students. Suggestions include reading rhythmic chants, creating raps using word spelling, and learning mathematics skills to a steady beat.
- Introduce new and difficult learning through all the perceptual modalities (vision, hearing, touch, kinesthetics, etc.) (Taylor, 1993)

At-risk students will participate more often if they are challenged, if they are accepted—without a value judgment—and if they are directed by an organized lesson.

Summary

Music and the other arts can be very beneficial for at-risk students in the following ways:

- *Socially.* Involvement in music activities and organizations can help students through difficult social situations, such as the first year of school at a new campus, by giving them a sense of group identity and belonging within the school.
- *Emotionally.* Music offers students an opportunity to express themselves, a way to release emotions that might otherwise be suppressed. Through music making, students can learn to think of themselves as valuable, successful people. Music also contributes to self-esteem, an improved attitude, and greater motivation for schoolwork.
- *Cognitively/academically.* Music study promotes creativity and can help students develop problem solving and critical-thinking skills, and it can be integrated across the curriculum to reinforce other subject matter. Students flourish in an arts-rich curriculum—using music within the curriculum helps make learning relevant and accessible for

students who have difficulty relating to traditional instruction.

Finally, it must be mentioned that not only do the music teachers and project directors featured in this chapter believe that music can reach—and has reached—the troubled student, they also believe that teachers must accept these high-risk students as individuals whose lives can be "turned around." This fact was eloquently stated by one of the music teachers: "Music is the channel for sparking hope in the dark lives of these [at-risk] children. However, the teacher who does not love, nor even tolerate, the high-risk child will reap no benefit from using music" (J. Cravath, personal communication, June 30, 1993). It is good to see a reminder that love for the students must be placed before all else.

Chapter 5

Perspectives from Music Professionals

Introduction

Many music educators have witnessed firsthand the power of music to turn around the direction of a young person's life. Thoughtful music professionals have considered how participation in music may have positive effects on the problem of at-risk students. Through their experiences and reflections, they have developed strategies for helping students who are at risk. In this section, a state music supervisor, a high school choral teacher, a high school band teacher, a middle school general music and band teacher, and several elementary school music teachers share their insights about how music can help students who are at risk.

A state music consultant speaks

June Hinckley is the music consultant for the state of Florida and president elect of MENC. She has been instrumental in bringing the needs of arts education—particularly music—to the attention of the Florida Department of Education. June Hinckley is a "doer." She makes a point of understanding educational processes in Florida by frequently visiting schools and talking to arts students, teachers, and administrators. Her perspective (which follows) on the values of music for at-risk children, then, is based upon firsthand observations and considerable thought about arts education for all students.

Why Music Is Essential to the Survival and Well-Being of the Child at Risk

"As the state music supervisor for almost 13 years of a state as large and diverse as Florida, I have had the opportunity to observe the macrochanges—good and bad—in music education over a period of time. Florida has had exponential growth during that period while dealing with the influx of refugees from Haiti, Cuba, and South America, as well as the Far East and Europe. According to social scientist Harold Hodgekinson, Florida is a bellwether state because it is a window to the future of America. Hodgekinson predicts that by the year 2010, white Americans will be in the minority. In Florida, almost forty percent of the student population consists of minority students. Although many schools have struggled with rapidly changing student demographics, the inner-city schools in large urban areas such as Miami, Ft. Lauderdale, Orlando, Jacksonville, and Tampa have had the greatest challenges. Florida has bemoaned its high dropout rate and tried many programs to better meet our diverse students' needs. In-services on teaching ESOL (English for Speakers of Other Languages) students are required of all Florida teachers. All textbook committees must look for multicultural representation in illustrations and text content. Most of the 'hot' issues in Florida, as with the rest of the nation, have been related to teaching students at risk of academic failure. We have alternative programs and outreach programs. We are implementing multiage grouping and adviser/advisee counseling. Innovation is the name of the game.

"While all schools have been hurt by the general nationwide reduction of state funding for education, the cruelest cuts of all have occurred in those schools that had the most needs and the least budgetary flexibility: large urban inner-city schools. In the area of music education, Florida has been lucky, although many music teachers would disagree. For the most part, despite the recent cutbacks in educational funding due to the recession, we have generally held onto music programs in our schools. We have, however, seen fine music programs perilously dwindle in student numbers because of the loss of the seven-period day in some school districts. Nevertheless, we have not been as hard hit as states in the northeast and industrialized midwest where budgetary crises have been going on for twenty years. City school systems like New York, Philadelphia, and Detroit, which at one time had enviable music programs, now have few or no programs at all.

"Of course, lack of funding was the basis for the loss of these programs, but the back-to-basics mentality, which supported cutting elective offerings for students who were not scoring well on standardized tests, contributed as well. Instead of capitalizing on students' strengths and interests, schools narrowed the curriculum and worked on remediating their weaknesses. The impact of the loss of funding and the narrowing of the instructional focus of education for impoverished children has been devastating. We have become less and less successful at teaching these students and have had fewer and fewer resources to make their schools interesting, exciting places. In Florida and nationwide, music programs in schools with the greatest concentration of disadvantaged students have struggled to survive, and the number of students at risk of dropping out of school keeps growing.

The Problems At-Risk Students Face

"When I was asked to write this section, I decided to review educational literature concerning at-risk children. I was struck by the shift in emphasis on problems associated with these young people. Topics of several years ago dealt with latchkey children, children of single parent homes, children at risk of academic failure because of alcohol or drug abuse, children of poverty, etc. Current literature, however, focuses on children infected with the AIDS virus, crack-affected children, children with fetal alcohol syndrome, the effects of lead poisoning on children's learning capabilities, and children of the homeless.

"Writers today are even more worried about how students who are at such great risk can develop the ability to organize new information and make sense of it, to achieve some social awareness and a sense of right and wrong, to trust others, and to perceive school as a safe place. They are concerned with how schools could intervene so that these children will become functional citizens in the adult world.

"The problems of latchkey children and children of poverty, and the risks of drug and alcohol abuse have not gone away. In fact, they have probably increased. They have simply been replaced as headline material by more life-threatening circumstances. The world has become a more violent and dangerous place for children. The major issue no longer is one of children staying in school. The real issue is their survival.

"Nowhere in the educational literature were the writers troubled that children might not have music and the other arts as a part of their schooling. Nowhere were they distressed that they may never come in contact with the concept of beauty. Nowhere were they concerned that they may never learn of their musical heritage. Because of the severity of today's problems it would be easy, even for us (as music educators), to buy into the idea that music and the other arts are of little concern in the inner city schools. In an overcrowded curriculum for children who in addition to learning the 'basics' must learn to survive in a dangerous world, what will study of the arts contribute to their intellectual, emotional, and physical development and well being?

Why is music essential to the child at risk?

"If we truly believe that music is an essential part of life, then we must believe it is essential for everyone. We must develop cogent arguments on the importance of music instruction for at-risk students. What skills can music and the arts offer these children that will contribute to their success and survival?

"The obvious answer is that the arts can offer what all children, not just the disadvantaged, need: the ability to deal with the ambiguity of today's world, the capacity to understand their past through their cultural heritage, and the power to transform their future and make it better.

"Elliot Eisner is professor of education and art at Stanford University and past president of the American Educational Research Association (AERA). He is frequently asked to be a spokesperson for the role of the arts in American education. Eisner (1992) presents the following four core contributions the arts make to further the aims of education. My suggested correlations for students at risk are also included:

- *Not all problems have single, correct answers.* Children at risk need to be creative and flexible to survive in a dangerous world. They need to learn to 'make do' in less-than-ideal circumstances, to make the best of bad situations when they can. Too much time in school centers around learning the single 'right' answer. The arts teach that there are many right answers. They celebrate multiple perspectives and personal interpretation. Children are encouraged in arts classes to take found objects and found sounds and transform them into things of beauty that have form and meaning. There are quite a few 'right' ways to sing a lullaby.

- *The form of a thing is part of its content.* Eisner says, "We have a tendency in our schools to separate form from content. Form is regarded as the shape something takes, and content is the meaning something conveys." Students learn in music that it is not only the notes that are played, but also the instruments that convey the inherent meaning of a blues tune or a Bach invention. In the arts, they are encouraged to look for the deeper message beyond the obvious. Why did the composer make the end of the musical phrase go up instead of down? Was it to convey a sense of hope and joy? On the streets, children must recognize hidden as well as purported meanings if they are to survive. In their world, the consequences of seeking simple solutions to problems may be fatal.

- *Having fixed objectives and pursuing clear-cut methods for achieving them are not always the most rational ways of dealing with the world.* The art of creation entails being open to chance. When a composer begins to write music, he or she cannot be absolutely certain how it will evolve. The process and circumstances of writing or performing a piece of music bring new ideas, interpretations, and choices to the musician. Even the youngest performers experience the difference an audience's response can make upon their performance. The arts encourage us to respond to the present and to stop and smell the roses. Children who are at risk often determine that they will never finish school, that they are doomed to be failures, and that they are powerless to change their destinies. Instead of pursuing courses of action that will ensure their success, they work to ensure their own failure by not attending school, acting out, not studying for tests, and associating with others who also see themselves as failures. Through the arts, these children may discover that they can change their destinies. They can use the skills they develop to solve artistic problems as alternative strategies for solving real-life problems. They can discover that artists can transform their world into a more beautiful, interesting, and provocative place. Many people who grew up in poverty and later became successful have identified a turning point in their lives when they decided to change their life script because of a chance association or opportunity that provided them with an alternative. For some, the arts provide these turning points.

- *Expression and discovery are two major contributions the arts make to human development.* By manipulating clay, interpreting a song, or acting in a play, students can 'find their individual capacity to feel and imagine. While such journeys are experiences through the arts, they also can be secured through the ordinary aspects of daily life when life is approached aesthetically. The world outside of art can become something to explore and relish... .' Children who are at risk too often do not have loved ones in their home environment to teach and nurture them. They must learn to do this for themselves if they are to survive. The world of imagination, creativity, and exploration provided in the arts as well as the skills of observation and attentiveness that the arts foster can spill over into all of life. Children who are observers of the world can learn from it (pp. 594–595).

"It is not enough to simply provide music instruction to students who are at risk. We must teach them in meaningful and successful ways. Means and Knapp (1991) have found the following instructional strategies to be successful with at-risk students:

- Focus on complex, meaningful problems.
- Embed basic skills instruction in the context of more global tasks.
- Make connections with students' out-of-school experiences and cultures.
- Encourage multiple approaches to academic tasks.
- Provide scaffolding to enable students to accomplish complex tasks.

- Make dialogue the central medium for teaching and learning (pp. 286–287).

"With the exception of the last strategy—and I think I could make a case for it through the Comprehensive Musicianship or Discipline-Based Arts Education models—all relate directly to the contributions Eisner suggests the arts make to human development. Because the arts reflect and affect all of human society, they can intersect with all educational experiences. The popular appeal of the arts sometimes allows them to be trivialized. It is up to us to ensure that arts instruction, whether it is being taught in a music or social studies class, focuses on 'meaningful, complex problems.'

"The highly touted SCANS Report (Secretary's Commission on Achieving Necessary Skills), distributed by the Department of Labor (1992), suggests another quality students need to be successful adults: self-discipline. Eisner does not directly refer to it as a skill learned through a study of the arts, but President Bill Clinton does. In the Allen and Portis book, *The Comeback Kid: The Life and Career of Bill Clinton* (1992), the president is quoted as believing that his experiences in the Hot Springs, Arkansas, band were some of the most important of his youth:

> All my musical competitions were great because it was so competitive, but, in a way, you were fighting against yourself. And music, to me, was—is—kind of representative of everything I like most in life. It's beautiful and fun but very rigorous. If you wanted to be good, you had to work like crazy. And it was a real relationship between effort and reward. My musical life experiences were just as important to me, in terms of forming my development, as my political experiences or my academic life. (p. 28)

The power of the arts

"President Clinton's experience with music was a life-changing one. Will all of America's children have this opportunity? How will our multiracial children ever learn of their musical heritage if we don't teach them? How will our children of poverty, abuse, crime, and illness ever learn about beauty if we do not teach it in school? Michael Greene, president of the National Academy of Recording Arts and Sciences, often voices his fear that music education for too many children today is provided by disk jockeys and MTV. He worries that young people are not hearing the great music of the

Western world. He is alarmed that they may never have the opportunity to experience their musical legacy of jazz or salsa or the blues. Too many students do not make musical choices because they do not know that the choices exist. Media icons may not make the best role models for young people; but unless schools and caring adults provide alternatives, television and popular culture will be their most powerful teachers.

"Young people who have been saved by the transforming power of the arts may offer the best arguments for the positive influence of the arts in the lives of students who are at risk. In a study by Barry, Taylor, and Walls (1990), at-risk students offer these reasons:

> 'It [music] has taught me that anything is possible; it may just take a greater amount of work and a greater commitment.'

> 'He [the student's band teacher] made it challenging; a place to learn not only music, but how to make something out of yourself, to be somebody.'

> 'In band, I learned not just about music but life, and how it really is in the big city.' (p. 40)

"Eisner (1992) suggests that 'providing a decent place for the arts in our schools may be one of the most important first steps we can take to bring about genuine school reform' (p. 592). We must speak up for those individuals who are too young or too impoverished to speak for themselves. We must, as a profession and a democratic society, be articulate and take on the fight for music and arts education for all students. We must believe that we have the potential to change lives, and we must act on that belief."

A high school choral teacher speaks

Dan Gordon has taught high school choral music in New York and Florida, and he recently earned a doctorate in music education at Florida State University. Presently, he is a member of the faculty at Christopher Newport College in Newport News, Virginia. Dan has worked extensively with at-risk students, and his efforts have led to considerable success in changing their negative attitudes toward school. His essay is based upon these experiences, particularly on the theme that arts and music classes offer an environment that can go a long way toward remediating problems of low self-esteem, lack of motivation, and poor attendance.

Music in the Schools: A Catalyst for Involving the Disenfranchised

"One of the primary missions of public schools is to equip students with the skills they need to succeed in contemporary society. Public school officials correctly recognize that food, shelter, clothing, and at least one adult advocate and supporter are necessary in the lives of all students if they expect to realize this educational mission. Federal and state subsidies including free and reduced-price school lunch, drop-out prevention programs, and a variety of counseling programs are intended to unburden at-risk students and provide them with equalizing services. These projects often continue indefinitely without being subjected to careful, objective review. Although these crisis intervention programs are initiated to combat student failures, lack of improved student performance is evidence that the basic needs of the at-risk population continue to be unfulfilled. Eventually, society bears the true expense of these failed attempts, and the community becomes the victim of the uneducated. Under circumstances where students' needs are left unmet, schools degenerate into what A. Bartlett Giamatti (1981) referred to as 'warehouses for the angry' (p. 157). William Glasser (1969) says:

> Giving up trying to become involved, they accept school as an impersonal place that does not contribute to fulfilling their needs. The motivated students react to the pain by trying harder; the others get rid of the pain by failing or dropping out. (pp. 218–219)

"Often, school activities help to fulfill the needs of at-risk students, providing a potential link to the schooling process. But this link can be severed swiftly by restrictive policies that ignore individual circumstances and cause students to disbelieve in a system presumably designed to meet their needs. Glasser (1969) continues:

> For talented students with good grades (that is, those who are allowed to participate), involvement in extracurricular activities somewhat makes up for the lack of involvement they have in regular classes. But it is the average and below-average student, even more than the successful one, who needs the personal contact with the faculty inherent in these activities. (p. 220)

"Glasser argues that schools eliminate students from extracurricular or cocurricular programs under the aegis of maintaining standards, even though these programs might be a student's only way to identify with success in school. Exclusionary "pass to play" policies that have been instituted by state legislatures and school boards throughout the country give little or no consideration to individual circumstances. Imagine the irreparable damage caused when such policies are applied uncompassionately. Should the pregnant 15-year-old be excluded from playing in the spring concert because absences affected her grades? Should the young man with an abusive father and codependent mother be eliminated from after-school music programs because he cannot concentrate in school? How important is algebra or general science to a student when he or she will face a drunken, maniacal father returning home from another day of looking for work? In these instances, students lose their relationship to school before that relationship can develop. Glasser (1969) concludes:

> Association with the better and more talented students increases the chance for [a student's] success. Because success in extracurricular activities (as well as in the academic program) is so highly related to involvement, we must try to get every student involved. (p. 220)

"The system's failure to involve at-risk students in school perpetuates behavior problems in classes. Further, the students experience what Csikszentmihalyi (1990) called 'psychic entropy'—the result of bad moods, lack of motivation, passivity, and unfocused attention (pp. 36–39). The symptoms of psychic entropy cause many educators to disassociate themselves with at-risk students. A well-organized school arts program, taught by knowledgeable, caring professionals, can combat psychic entropy and pave the road to the student's re-involvement in school. Unfortunately, arts programs are often the last to be funded and the first to be eliminated when funding shrinks. Even when present in the curriculum, the value of arts education is often misunderstood and de-emphasized. Therefore, arts educators experience frustrations in school similar to those of the at-risk students. Ironically, the system fails to help at-risk students by failing to support and understand dynamic arts programs in schools.

"Scholars and aestheticians vigorously assert music's pivotal position in the school curriculum. Harry S. Broudy (1988) suggests that the arts are more difficult to explain; as a result, their place in the curriculum is separated from more concrete disciplines. He says:

The mystique of art has been the source of wonder and awe. In schooling, it has meant a division between the arts and the academic subjects that has prevented the arts from achieving a permanent place in the roster of studies required for general education. (p. 61)

"Broudy presents three arguments that substantiate the place of art in the school's core curriculum. First, he believes that the aesthetic experience is a unique and powerful phenomenon. The capacity to experience art aesthetically stimulates intellectual growth and feeds the human spirit in ways not found in other areas of the curriculum. Highly trained, specialized teachers should facilitate perception of art and its aesthetic qualities. Broudy suggests that imagery nurtured in effective arts programs enables students to become insightful, imaginative people, capable of solving difficult problems and inventing new ways of approaching life. Finally, Broudy believes that the discipline inherent to success in the arts is essential to a complete education. When individual and group discipline result in personal gratification, the benefits of working 'for the good of the group' become apparent. This manifestation of group discipline contains powerful implications for participation in a democratic society.

"Our national preoccupation with student performance on standardized tests has diminished enrollment in arts classes. Standardized tests no longer exist as diagnostic tools, but as the primary yardstick with which we measure school accountability. Entire courses are developed to help students "pass the test." Some electives must be eliminated from the struggling student's course of study to make room for such remedial classes. An arts class is often the first to go.

"Elliot Eisner (1985) believes that our bottom-line mentality regarding testing does more harm than good. Another factor that undermines the aesthetic is that the rewards that are emphasized in class are rewards emanating from test performance. What far too many teachers and students care about almost solely is how well they do on tests. Again, the focus is on the short term and the instrumental. Yet the enduring outcomes of education are to be found in consummatory satisfaction—the joy of the ride, not simply arriving at the destination. If the major satisfaction in schools are high test scores, the value of what is learned tends to decline precipitously after the tests are taken. The only confident way to have a bull market in schooling is to turn students on to the satisfactions of inquiry in the fields into which they are initiated (p. 34). Eisner's 'joy of the ride' becomes more potent when applied to the school music ensemble, where a skilled music teacher can facilitate the transformation of music notation into aural magic. More often than not, the rehearsal process is sprinkled with wonder, suggestions of what could be, and moments of utter beauty. These moments can provide a new raison d'être for the at-risk student; no test can accurately measure its meaning to the individual, and no academic alternative can replace it in the curriculum. When it is gone from the student's course of study, it is gone forever.

"Music educators are left with several challenges. First, we must convince those who exert the greatest influence upon education that we have a core curricular subject from which all students benefit. The place of music in the curriculum must transcend school spirit and positive public relations. Second, we must lead students to the kinds of personal and group musical experiences that are an integral part of the human experience. Music programs that rightfully 'start where the students are' but never address the subtle, expressive, and complex aspects of music confirm the suspicions of those who relegate music courses to a secondary role in the curriculum. Finally and ultimately, the music teacher must personalize the curriculum for students from a variety of backgrounds to feel empowered to discover, appreciate, experience, and respond to music in their unique way, while developing the group music-making potential of the entire class. The ensemble director must provide a safe, failure-proof environment that includes music of various cultures and styles. The lessons must challenge students whose ability lies in all dimensions of Bruner's (1960) spiral curriculum (p. 52).

"Effective in-service training, local decision-making power, alternative assessment strategies, and interdisciplinary instruction have become familiar terms in the educational reform movement. MENC offers the most comprehensive and effective in-service training available in American education. This organization sponsors national and regional conventions directed at its grassroots membership, providing them with an opportunity to obtain the knowledge needed to make effective decisions at the local level. Reformers, recognizing that objective tests are being misused, urge educators to develop alternative assessment strategies like portfolios, projects, and oral examinations. Arts educators have used these procedures effectively for generations. Interdisciplinary instruction is needed to teach the transfer of knowledge and to emphasize the relevance among subjects. Music teachers, who have understood the benefits of this strategy for years, often provide resources for those who teach subjects that seem unrelated to music. Additionally, which music teacher has not taught mathematic, scientific, historic, and linguistic concepts? Perhaps the forward-thinking strategies used in arts education should be recognized as appropriate models for effective instruction.

"American business executives have frequently complained that their competitive edge has diminished in part thanks to an unprepared work force. The United States Department of Labor formed the Secretary's Commission on Achieving Necessary Skills (SCANS) in 1992 to develop a list of skills students must acquire to enter employment. Further, the commission was asked to propose proficiency levels and means of assessment for the basic skills they identify. Creative thinking, decision making, problem solving, seeing things in the mind's eye, self-esteem, sociability, self-management, teamwork, monitors and corrects performance, interprets and communicates information, and works with diversity were among the skills named. Each of these skills can be addressed daily in performing arts classes, while nearly all of the other five competencies and three foundations mentioned in the report are accessible through the arts.

"Solid school music programs are purveyors of the essential skills identified in the SCANS report and can be the link between at-risk students and the acquisition of these skills. At-risk students need to develop critical-thinking skills. There are no courses in the school curriculum that demand the number of immediate decisions involving specific cognitive, affective, and psychomotor responses simultaneously like music. At-risk students need to develop a positive self-image. Since music ensembles produce no losers, only participants, that try to recreate a composer's intentions, students get to win through aesthetic satisfaction. Self-image can improve greatly in artistic circumstances. At-risk students need to learn the value of teamwork. Many students gain this experience in team sports, but victory and defeat become the measure of success. Teamwork designed to achieve artistic perfection demands flexibility and consistency. Musicians struggle for the perfect phrase only to meet with their own limitations, which inspires more careful practice and the search for greater understanding. This manifestation of teamwork draws people together and closely resembles the kind of cooperation needed for success in the real world. Effective music teachers demand that students monitor and correct their performance constantly in rehearsals. The development of this skill is central to any successful music rehearsal. At-risk students need so much from school, and music has so much to offer them.

"Music's value is both pragmatic and esoteric. Music classes can help students develop skills relevant to entering the work force, while elevating and inspiring the humanness of each individual. Given its proper place in the curriculum, music can be the magical intervention strategy that encourages students to learn in school.

"Many students stay in school and receive a diploma because they discovered a new world in a music classroom. The powers of imagination they develop give birth to a vision of self-actualization. The intimacy and family atmosphere of a music class fulfill unmet needs from a troubled home life. Undoubtedly, the opportunity to create music with others is magnetic and at-risk students all over America will continue to be attracted. Music teachers, administrators, students, parents, and community members should comprehend the potential for a positive outcome when music resides at the heart of the curriculum. If all our children, rich or poor, preschoolers or college students, were given access to quality music instruction throughout their school careers, the number of citizens who plead for educational reform would diminish greatly."

A high school instrumental teacher speaks

The following is an excerpt from an interview with Curtis Hollinger, band director for more than twenty years at Carver High School in Montgomery, Alabama. Carver High School is one of the larger predominantly black high schools in the state. Hollinger is highly respected by his professional peers for his excellent musicianship (he is the principal clarinetist with the Montgomery Symphony Orchestra) and teaching. He has been a constant source of inspiration and information for younger band directors in Montgomery and central Alabama. Under Hollinger's guidance, the Carver band has been consistently noted for its musicality in performing challenging concert literature. His comments offer excellent advice for all teachers, as well as for music educators; furthermore, they are applicable to all students (not only those who are at risk).

Do you remember any situations when music study helped at-risk students to stay in school?

"Band encourages students to stay in school; however, you don't get them all to stay. What we do in band encourages them to stay in school and develop good work habits. It makes them better people all around. Our band program really doesn't attract many at-risk students (about five percent are at risk).

"I can't think of band students [at Carver High School] who have dropped out of school permanently. But we've had two or three girls who became pregnant and dropped out of school for awhile. The girls returned to school and graduated. One of them eventually got her master's degree.

"There was a boy who said he was going to college, but I thought he was not putting enough into high school. He did go to college, got a master's degree, and eventually played in the Army band in Washington, D.C.

"One boy did not graduate on time in May, but came back in the summer and finished school. He eventually got his college degree and went on to become a band director. He was not a bad student; he just didn't do all he could do in his classes and came up a little bit short. But he's done well overall.

"We try to teach the students in band to work hard to achieve their goals and not to give up when things get tough. Maybe they carry this over into their lives."

What is it about your band program that encourages students to stay in school?

"Music comes first, but it's not the only thing I teach in band class. First of all, I try to get to know all the students and to learn something about their backgrounds, so that I can have some understanding of how they think and what their values are. Then I have to try to teach them why my values are worth trying—or worthwhile for them to make my values a part of their lives. Once I know something about my students, it's easier for me to do that."

So you would advise music educators to teach serious literature instead of pop music?

"Absolutely! Tell them why it is important for them to learn it. Then teach it, whether they take it positively or not, because later on in their lives they will. When they come to school, they don't know what they should learn, and that's why we're there. They're not there to have fun, they've come for an education. The best thing to do is to understand them, let them understand you, and then tell them why, show them why, and teach them music whether they like it or not."

What do you expect from your at-risk students?

"I expect a lot from my students. One of the things I tell the students is that if they cannot be good musicians, they must be good citizens. All of them are not going to be good musicians, but all of them can be good people.

"You have to explain to students why it is important to be well-disciplined. I tell students that they must sit down and be quiet and attentive—not because they're afraid of me, but because they're intelligent. That gives them a sense of worth. Once they know that they're doing it because they are intelligent, not because they are afraid of you, then they patrol themselves."

Do you remember any students who were at risk of dropping out of school, yet were successful in music?

"I had a student who was educable disabled who eventually learned to read music, but had a terrible time with it. I think that no one sat down with him to teach him how to read. I tutored him in my office. He did graduate.

"I had a boy this past year who is going to be a music major in college. He didn't do well in English and his teacher was always telling me about it. Of course I would counsel him and tell him to listen to his teacher, because she was trying to help him. If a teacher counsels you, takes the time to talk to you, or gets on you about not doing your best, it means that the teacher cares about you. When a teacher doesn't say anything to you and knows that you're not doing all that you can do, that teacher doesn't care. I don't know how much good my counseling did, but he graduated. I've always felt that we [music educators] do so much, so many things, although we're usually the only music teacher and have more students than anybody else. The teachers in the rest of the school should look into the arts and see what it is that we do to get success— it is not easy to learn all the things that a musician has to. If we can teach students to play an instrument, to learn and read the names of notes, to read rhythms, to learn expression, to learn fingerings, and to work together, we should be able to teach them how to read and write."

Is the group effort emphasized in your classes?

"Yes, we expect everybody to do his or her best to make our organization as good as it can be. Our band has been able to earn superior ratings at district festivals because some students help the weaker ones. They actually become my assistants. All the section leaders and upper-class players are paired off with a tenth grader to help them learn their music.

"They teach them the fingerings that I previously had to teach them. That way the students have a real sense of belonging. I offer the leadership, the teaching, and the advice, and the students help each other, making for a really close-knit group. The kids respect each other and they respect authority, no matter whether it's me on the podium or anybody else—because I demand it."

What do you do to keep at-risk students in your program?

"You have to do things now to compete with other organizations. To help with the transition from junior high school to high school we have a spring band clinic in March. I spend a week with the students so that they can get to know me, become familiar with our system, and get to know their fellow bandsmen that they will be with next year. Some of them are afraid that I am really a tyrant until they get to know that I just mean business. Then I have no problems.

"Another thing I do is to take them on trips. I don't emphasize contests—we go to one marching contest—and I take them to Florida. I plan to take them to Washington, D.C., next year and also to Williamsburg, Virginia. We want trips to be fun, but educational, which we emphasize to them."

Is there any other advice you would give music educators that would help keep students in school?

"The best thing to do is to show students that you really care about them. Students are smart. They can see right through you, and they are smart enough to know when you are honest or when you're not sincere. If they know that you are serious about what you're doing and that you genuinely care about your subject matter, they develop respect for you and will do almost anything you ask.

"Be totally honest and fair. You can't treat them all the same; you can't talk to each of them the same way, but you can have rules that apply to everyone. Once you enforce the rules with one person, you have to do the same with the others. When they see that you're not going to show preferences, they respect you even more, even though they may not like you."

A middle school band teacher speaks

The following is an interview with Danny Lopez, the band director at Rhodes Middle School. Rhodes is a small, predominantly Mexican-American middle school in one of the poorer districts of San Antonio, Texas. Mr. Lopez has been teaching band at Rhodes for more than 15 years and has also instituted a mariachi program in the school. He is an active participant in the San Antonio music community—playing horn in several community bands—and has built his career around meeting the needs of low-income, inner-city Hispanic youth.

Please describe your school.

"Rhodes Middle School has about 500 to 550 students. It's an inner-city middle school in the San Antonio Independent School District. It has grades six through eight and serves a part of the city that would be characterized as low on the socioeconomic scale. About 90–95% of the kids enrolled at the school are on the free lunch program. I would say that the vast majority of them are at-risk students."

Does your school have special programs for at-risk students?

"Yes, there's an at-risk committee for each grade. I don't serve on any at-risk committees, but I'm on the campus site-based management committee. Our committee has not had any input into how the school's at-risk program is managed, but it's possible that we might in the future."

What kind of interventions or programs do the at-risk committees sponsor?

"They have incentive programs where they'll give prizes to kids who improve their attendance and things like that. The prizes are available if you ask for them. I've not done that because I usually do it on my own through fund-raising or something similar."

What kinds of things do you reward in your music classes?

"I give prizes, especially for participation. I find that the kids are very insecure. The basic problem is their lack of confidence. Every day I hear, 'I can't do it' or 'I'll never be able to do this,' especially about performances. You'd think they'd want to perform, but they seem unwilling. It's strange, but when I announce a performance, I hear a lot of, 'Well, I'm not going' and 'I can't make it.' I have to do something to get them into the mind-set to perform. Once they perform, their confidence improves, but their low self-esteem makes them afraid that they will mess up. For example, on one occasion I wanted to play at a mall for Christmas. We had never done that before. When I told the kids we were invited to play, one of them said, 'Why would they want a school from Westside to play at the mall?' When that happened, I knew we *had* to play. So now we play at a mall every year to let the band students know they're just as good as anybody else. I've done some Sunday School work at my church with high school seniors, and they were the same way. They were from another poor school district and were afraid to go to college to compete with kids from other school districts. They just don't feel that they're good enough."

How do you build their self-esteem?

"Every time my beginners perform, I videotape them and show them the tape right away. Many people are visually oriented instead of aurally oriented, so I make it a point that they see themselves every time they perform. I think it helps. When they hear themselves making mistakes, I tell them 'Hey, it's normal to make mistakes; don't worry about it.' Even if I drill them on something in class, some students tell me, 'I don't want to do it' just because they're afraid of making a mistake. It happens in every class. But the kids are just as good as any other kids in any other school. It's just that they don't think they are."

Do you ever have students who need financial help with buying instruments?

"Yes. I have students who can't even buy the black pants and white shirt that belong with their uniform. I've had to loan them money for that. I've had students who have trouble just buying a reed."

Are the parents involved in your program?

"We don't have a parents' organization, but parents are somewhat involved. They provide rides when we play at an elementary school. I have parents who tell me, 'Anytime you need something, let me know.' We have fund-raisers in which many parents take candy forms to work to collect orders. I've never had a parent tell me 'No.'

You've been able to follow many students as they progress to the high school and graduate. Do you recall any at-risk students who were helped to stay in school and to graduate because of their involvement in music?

"I can't think of a time a student [from our high school] has told me, 'Sir, because I was in music, I graduated from high school.' But I know of students in other schools where that has happened."

How many of your junior high school students sign up for high school band?

"The majority of the kids. With House Bill 72 ('no pass, no play'), a lot of them know that they're not going to play anyway. I have kids who have been in the middle school band program, yet they've never performed because they're always failing. So they say, 'Well, I'm never going to be in a halftime show,' because they know they're going to fail when they go to high school. I've had kids who have gone through the program and who've never performed at all."

What are the specific restrictions of House Bill 72?

"If you make a 70 score or below in any class, you cannot perform for the next six weeks, period. If you raise your grade on the next report card, then you can perform. So if you keep failing every six weeks, you never get to perform. I have a student who passed for the first time this past six weeks. I told him, 'Now you're going to get to play with us.' He looked at me as if to say, 'I don't know if I want to play. I've never played before.' So now I've got to build his confidence and make sure he can play."

What other things do you do to build the students' confidence?

"I like to talk to them in private, because they tend to get really embarrassed when you mention their name in class. First, I find out if they're receptive to having their names mentioned. Then, I praise them in class—once or twice, but not too often. I speak to them between classes, or before or after school."

Describe your music classes.

"I have sixth-, seventh-, and eighth-grade bands for five periods, and I have one general music class, which is really the mariachi class. Since mariachi isn't a UIL [University Interscholastic League, the state agency that oversees athletic and music competitions] activity, all the kids can perform in that class. So whenever we have an assembly for which the mariachi is scheduled to perform, they all perform, whether or not they are passing."

"Yes."

Do you think that band and mariachi have different effects on at-risk students?

"I think so. At Rhodes, mariachi is not an elective, per se. The kids do not elect to be in mariachi. Kids who did not sign up for band either get put in homemaking, or general music, or art, or something like that. It just so happens that we have said, 'All right, the general music class is going to become the mariachi class.' We ask the kids which instruments they'd like to play. [These instruments are provided by the school.] The program eventually will feed into a high school mariachi program, although it's only a sixth-grade program right now. We are trying to make an elective of mariachi in the seventh and eighth grades. Mariachi is only a one-semester class, but we've had some kids from the first semester who have elected to stay in for a second semester. So apparently, they enjoy it. Right now, we have about 30 kids in the class."

Do you think that since your students are more familiar with mariachi music than band literature, that mariachi is more successful in reaching at-risk students?

"Yes, I think the students are more familiar with mariachi music. All of my kids have probably seen mariachi from the time they are small. In San Antonio, it's traditional at every wedding to have a mariachi. You really don't see bands that often unless you go to a high school football game or a college football game—and my kids ordinarily don't go to college football games or concerts.

"My kids don't know a lot of the folk songs in the beginning band books. They're inner-city people and they don't know 'Go Tell Aunt Rhody.' Tell them to sing the song and it's just another new song. They've never heard it before because it's not part of their culture. For my kids, music education really is multicultural because they learn the words to songs of other cultures."

Does music help students stay in school more than some of the other disciplines do?

"Music in and of itself doesn't. It's the teacher that's going to make the difference. You could teach Bach or M. C. Hammer, but if your kids can't connect with you, it's not going to help. So I think a lot of it has to do with personality and people. If you have an English teacher who's a wonderful person and the kids love her or him—and if that person is involved in stage plays—that might be more valuable to students [than music]. Of course, as a musician, I want to say that music alone can do it. I'm a band director because of the music.

"I think you've got to reach at-risk kids at their level. If they get involved with the music, they'll love it, because everybody loves music. But you've got to start with "their" music. You've got to find out what kids are listening to, and then use that music in class."

What are some other techniques a music teacher can use to reach the at-risk student?

"Clifford Madsen [author of the book *Teaching/Discipline: Behavioral Principles toward a Positive Approach* (Contemporary Publishing, Inc., 1983)] has said that the ideal ratio of positive to negative reinforcement should be 80% to 20%. When I started teaching, there was a lot of negativity in my efforts to be demanding. Other teachers told me, 'Danny, you've got to demand the best all the time—don't let the kids set the tempo.' But I'm really beginning to understand that you've got to accentuate the positive as much as possible and focus on what the kids are doing well. You do have to be demanding, you've got to have standards, and the kids have to know what they can get away with and what they can't. At least where I teach, you've got to accentuate the positive because these kids already have a lot of negative feelings about themselves."

What advice would you give to music teachers who want to help at-risk students?

"Every time you talk to parents, tell them the way things are [regarding their child] and be honest with them. I have meetings with every parent with his or her child present. We've tried out instruments and discussed the best one(s) for the child. The parents know exactly what we've done and exactly what they need to do. The involvement of the parents is the most important thing. If the parents would sit down and listen to their child for five minutes, that's probably a bigger incentive than any prize I could give the student. If the parent says, 'That's great, you're a really good player,' that's probably more important than anything I give them. I tell this to the parents, both in person and in a letter from 'The Essential Elements' [band method], which I've translated into Spanish.

Just about every letter I send is bilingual because many parents don't speak English. Also, many parents don't know what an appointment is. When you call them and ask for an appointment to try instruments out, they don't understand what you mean when you set a specific time. They'll say, for example, 'Well, I can be there in the afternoon.'

"I'd also tell teachers to have a lot of patience, especially with discipline. Often, kids will misbehave because they want your attention. They don't necessarily want praise from you, they just want any attention you'll give them. This happens in every class. Also, it's especially difficult to get kids to want to do 'fun' things. They don't want to appear vulnerable. They want to look strong all the time—like they're in control.

"I have another suggestion for teachers: Don't be afraid to ask questions of someone else. Don't be afraid to network. I know that was one of my biggest problems when I started teaching, but other people are always willing to help. Music teachers are very isolated. That's why I started playing with the municipal band: to meet other people and to listen to them."

Elementary school general music teachers speak

Ten San Antonio, Texas, elementary school music teachers participated in an in-service session on "Music and the At-Risk Student." As part of their participation, they completed written survey forms and discussed their experiences with at-risk students in the music classroom. The following are excerpts from their surveys and discussion. The session included supervisor Leo Greene and music teachers Rhonda Blakely, Merie Skinner, Rosanna Helsel, Winnie Harvin, Judy Gorrell, Laura Hall, Linda Gomez Richter, Tamara Bell, Sandy Musk, and Brian O. Achles.

Every teacher indicated that his or her music classes included at-risk students. Several teachers commented that they were not informed about who was at risk in their classes because remediation efforts were concentrated in the academic subjects. Yet all teachers agreed that participation in their music classes had encouraged at-risk students to stay in school.

The teachers were asked how their music classes benefited at-risk students. Their replies were revealing:

■ "Sometimes it's the only subject area in which they feel 'special.' They're proud of what they're able to accomplish. They can 'start over' in music if they've had a bad day or if they don't have a good relationship with their classroom teacher."

■ "Successful participation in performing groups makes them want to come to school."

■ "Performing makes students feel successful, which boosts their self-esteem."

■ "Music participation helps students to cooperate with other students and takes away their feeling of aloneness. It gives them an interest or activity so they don't have to look to gangs for fun and involvement."

■ "I have many at-risk students every year who surprise me by saying they've joined band, orchestra, or choir—I had never thought they would do that."

■ "Some of these children have expressed a desire for a career in music; some have indicated that feelings of peace and happiness happen with music."

■ "Music participation builds self-esteem, enjoyment of a learning process that they can relate to, holistic teaching practices that cater to the whole child and thus nurture them. Music creates a 'safe' environment for learning and interacting with others."

■ "It makes the children feel better about themselves. If they have a part in the choir, they'll want to come to school."

■ "Unconscious skills are learned in listening and in being part of a group. Students come to realize that a person may not have wonderful skills in all areas."

The teachers also contributed advice about how music teachers may help at-risk students:

■ "Praise, praise, praise! Praise them personally and to other teachers and to their parents. Give them opportunities in class to shine."

■ "Concentrate on success-oriented assignments and activities."

■ "Try to ensure success; accentuate the positive."

■ "Music teachers should provide a warm, stimulating, and secure learning environment for their students. They should make each student feel that his or her contributions are special."

■ "Don't give up trying to sell your program and telling

them all the fun things that happen in middle and high
school. Be willing to stay after school and visit with
them."
- "Find the child's strength and reinforce it—whether it's singing, dancing, or just listening."
- "Use many different activities to reach as many students as possible."
- "Allow them to create their own music using the concepts they've learned in class."
- "Encourage and highlight their own responses. Help them be aware of their own reactions and feelings."
- "Give at-risk students your attention, even more than you'd give a student who's not at risk. Go the extra mile. Compliment them often, pat them on the back. Tell them you've enjoyed having them in your class."
- "My synthesizer has helped me interest some students who didn't find anything else interesting in my room."
- "Make them feel important in your class."
- "Be genuine."

The teachers also thought that music might help at-risk
students more than some other subjects:
- "Music requires self-discipline, but at the same time, it's pleasurable. It touches every student down deep inside so that the inexpressible can be expressed."
- "Music requires focus and active, conscious control of behavior in a more self-disciplined way than other disciplines."
- "Music is less grade oriented, which leads to less stress."
- "Music adds fun to learning and lends itself to a variety of activities."
- "Students need good listening skills, which are acquired through music classes. This carries over into regular classrooms—they're able to concentrate better."
- "Music might reach students who have problems with reading."
- "Music evokes emotions that other disciplines may not. The emotional connection can be an avenue to tap into the child's feelings or problems. The child may 'open up' more to a music teacher because he or she sees emotion displayed in a positive way—a 'safe' way. The sheer

enjoyment of a group process may be an experience the
student hasn't had before."

■ "Music appeals to the very soul. Sometimes, it's the only
thing that makes these children feel good all day."

Summary

June Hinckley observes that students today are at even
greater risk than their predecessors. Today, the real issue is
survival. Thus, it becomes even more crucial that teachers and
parents cooperate in protecting and promoting both the social
and educational welfare of their children. Children at risk have
already fallen prey to some of the undesirable effects of mod-
ern society, and it becomes especially important that we, as
music teachers, make strong, positive connections between
these students and their parents. Danny Lopez has discovered
the value of these connections with his at-risk middle school
children, and he also notes that music teachers must network
with other teachers both in the same school and elsewhere.
Peer influence can be added to the parent-teacher-student mix.
Using older, more secure band students as mentors to the
younger (and perhaps at-risk) students, Curtis Hollinger has
found that discipline problems decrease and that students learn
to respect each other.

It is important to realize that students at risk can lose their
relationship to school before that relationship can develop.
Dan Gordon observed that teachers sometimes contribute to
this problem by disassociating themselves from at-risk students. Arts teachers can avoid this problem by welcoming the
hesitant student to their classes. The elementary school general
music teachers interviewed for this book emphasized the fact
that performing makes students feel special, thus boosting
their self-esteem and connections to their classmates and
teachers. Furthermore, the arts require considerable self-discipline, while at the same time being fun. Perhaps, in the long
term, the essence of music is its ability to satisfy the need for
aesthetic expression.

Why are we concerned about the study of the arts when
the basic issue at hand for these students is survival? Because
children need to be creative and flexible to survive in a dangerous world. Music and the arts provide the ability to deal
with the ambiguity of today's world, the capacity to under-

stand the past through one's cultural heritage, and the power to transform the future and make it better. Through the study of the arts, children can be encouraged to seek deeper meanings. Having fixed objectives and methods is not always the most rational way of dealing with the world.

Chapter 6

Summary and Conclusions

Summary

The at-risk problem is extensive, with an increasingly large percentage of youth throughout the nation being at risk of failure in school and in life. The at-risk phenomenon is pervasive and has negative ramifications that are evident throughout a student's life; it also has damaging effects upon all of society. The at-risk problem is a costly dilemma and exacts a high toll upon our country both economically and emotionally.

We are all affected by the problem of students at risk in some way, but for those working with young people, the issues become particularly acute. Music and arts teachers are not immune to these problems. There are at-risk students in music and arts classes just as there are at-risk students in other classes. It would be easy for arts teachers to discourage troubled students from taking their classes (after all, at-risk students often exhibit behavior problems that make them challenging to work with), but it is important for music and arts teachers to recognize that they are in a unique position to help troubled students overcome some of the negative feelings (such as self-doubt and alienation) that lead to at-risk attitudes and behaviors.

Many different factors in different combinations place students at risk. These factors generally fall into two broad categories: (1) descriptive characteristics, which are situations and/or circumstances that are often beyond the child's control, and (2) high-risk behaviors, in which the child's actions contribute to the problem. Each situation is unique, but we can identify certain characteristics and behaviors such as social and economic disadvantage and low academic achievement (the descriptive characteristics most frequently associated with at-risk behaviors) as early warning signs that enable us to provide appropriate intervention.

Because risk tends to be pervasive, engulfing many aspects of a child's life, successful intervention programs must involve all areas of the curriculum and extend into the home and community. Parental involvement is essential. Successful intervention programs set high expectations for students and provide individualized attention. Interaction with other students, as in mentoring and peer tutoring programs, is also effective.

Music educators can make a difference in the lives of at-risk children. When the arts are integrated with other subjects in an interdisciplinary manner, school becomes more meaningful and is perceived as a coherent whole, rather than a succession of nonrelated activities. Children are more motivated when music and the arts are part of their school day.

One of the characteristics associated with students at risk is a feeling of alienation, of not fitting into the school environment. Programs such as ability tracking and "no pass, no play" rules tend to exacerbate the problem by denying at-risk students associations with achievers. Inclusive policies that allow all children to participate together promote a sense of belonging. The esprit de corps evident in many musical performing groups can lead to changes in the at-risk student's negative attitudes about self and school, breaking the cycle of helplessness and anger that pervades the attitudes of many underprivileged children.

Participation in music and other arts classes provides opportunities for self-expression and creativity that are generally not available in other classes. Learning to communicate and solve problems through music and the other arts can equip at-risk students with creative ways of responding to a dangerous and uncertain environment. The discipline required to succeed in arts activities can carry over into other areas, which helps at-risk students set and meet goals in school and in life. Cognitive skills such as critical thinking and problem-solving strategies developed through arts experiences are applicable to other academic subjects.

Conclusions

We acknowledge that each community and school represents a unique combination of resources and challenges. What works in one situation may not be effective in a different setting. However, our research has revealed that there are certain basic aspects that are common to all successful intervention programs. While not intended as a specific outline for developing a successful program, the following recommendations can provide a useful starting point for music educators interested in addressing the needs of at-risk students.

Change cannot occur without student motivation. Intervention programs can be successful only if students are motivated to change their at-risk attitudes and behaviors. Dryfoos (1990) explains that first students must want to learn, then they have to realize the importance of these learnings to their lives. Music and the other arts are intrinsically motivating to many students and actively involve students in the learning process and in the school environment.

Effective intervention begins early. Rarely does a solitary factor place a child at risk. At-risk children tend to be victims of combinations of situations and circumstances that create a chain of disappointments and failures. Failure breeds failure, and the child spirals toward ultimate disaster unless something is done. Early intervention enables us to break the tragic chain of failures before irreparable damage has been done. Music educators must address individual student needs in the early grades. Upper-level music teachers can begin working with younger students even before they enter their programs by visiting feeder school music classes, making friends toward other music teachers, and getting to know the younger students and their parents.

Self-esteem must be addressed. Even when students value learning, they may not attempt academic achievement if they are convinced that they will not succeed. Many students learn that it is "safer" to refuse to try something new than to risk the humiliation of yet another failure. Arts activities are well suited

for increasing at-risk students' self-esteem. They involve a variety of sensory learning modes and give students opportunities
to be successful in ways that are not typically available in other
courses. Successful experiences in music and the other arts can
build student confidence and pride in accomplishment. As self-
esteem increases, the positive ramifications can carry over into
other situations.

Teacher consistency is essential. Teachers who are perceived as caring, fair, consistent, and nonjudgmental attract the
respect and loyalty of their students. For some children, the
teacher is the only stable and dependable adult in their lives.

High expectations must be maintained. Teachers who
demand excellence while maintaining a nurturing and supportive environment tend to bring out the best in students. It is
important to maintain high standards and insist that each child
do his or her best. To demand less gives the child clear signals
that he or she is incapable of achieving at the same level as
other children. High expectations are evident when musically
challenging literature is selected. Solo award selections and
ensemble audition results must be gender and culture sensitive.
Although performance standards must be upheld, we must be
careful to avoid situations that tend to reinforce negative feelings that students may already have about themselves.
Competition and ability tracking should be deemphasized,
especially in the lower grades. Students should see evidence
that economic advantage and a rich musical background are
not the sole determinants of successful musical performance.
Music educators must put forth an extra effort to ensure that
students from poor backgrounds may achieve excellent musicianship.

*Individualization is important because each child is
unique.* Students can express themselves in unique and personal ways through the arts. At-risk students need to know that
they can produce something of value. They need opportunities
to affirm their worth as individuals. The importance of each
student may be emphasized by stressing his or her contribution
to the ensemble and by giving praise and approval not only to
talented students, but also to those who strive for musical
growth.

Parental involvement is important. Parental involvement
and support are essential elements in successful intervention
programs for troubled students. Parents must be enlisted as
"full partners in the education of their children" (Dougherty,
1990, p. 34). Unfortunately, parents often view school staff in
an adversarial role, but the arts can help generate parental sup-

port. Student performances and art shows at school and in the community allow parents, school staff, and students to come together in a positive and supportive setting that emphasizes student accomplishments.

Peer influence is powerful. Peers exert a powerful influence on young people, an influence that is often much more powerful than the adult influences in their lives. Through the arts, students from diverse backgrounds can interact. In performing ensembles, low-achieving and high-achieving students can work together as a team in which each member makes a valuable contribution. No-pass, no-play rules remove students who are experiencing failure from performing groups and separate them from peers who are positive role models.

Cultural differences. One reason that many students drop out of school and mainstream society is that they do not perceive the things in mainstream society as being relevant to their own culture. We cannot assume that all minority students want to join the mainstream. Some students may choose to fail because they do not want to be perceived as trying to fit into a culture that differs from that of their family and friends (Ogbu, 1992). Arts courses are a wonderful place for students to learn about and appreciate their own culture and other cultures. A student may be penalized for using nonstandard English in a language arts course, but in music and in the other arts, modes of expression from diverse cultures are equally valid. Music programs that include performing groups representing diverse cultures (such as a gospel choir or a mariachi band) foster respect and understanding among students from different cultural backgrounds.

Effective programs are comprehensive. Because risk is such a pervasive element in the lives of most at-risk children, it would be naive to assume that "band-aid" solutions addressing only some aspects of the child's life can be effective. Limited programs tend to produce limited results. The most effective programs are comprehensive and address students' needs at school, at home, and in the community. The arts can be a starting point for positive interactions within the home— they give parents a reason to feel proud of their children. The arts can facilitate positive school/community relations and can make student achievements visible within the community.

Strategies for teachers. Research and practice indicate that participation in arts experiences can be an effective intervention strategy for decreasing certain high-risk student behaviors. Many music educators can attest to firsthand experiences with students whose academic and/or personal lives got "turned around" as a result of positive experiences in band, chorus, guitar class, orchestra, or another music class. Music classes provide some troubled young people with their only taste of success during the school day and a rare opportunity to assume a position of leadership and trust within the school environment. Yet research and practice also point out that at-risk students may also be capable of giving the teacher much trouble; difficulty in interacting with authority figures and a history of discipline problems are characteristics that are frequently observed in at-risk students. Those students who need our help the most may be the ones who seem the least willing to accept it. For this reason, teachers must be equipped with strategies for dealing with difficult students. Allen's (1991) list of suggestions for defusing angry students could prove useful when a situation becomes tense:

- Take care of yourself—you personally need to survive and thrive.
- Remember, students are responsible for their own behavior.
- Try to understand what motivates the at-risk student.
- Deal with one specific behavior at a time, not the whole personality.
- Allow yourself to enjoy the small chunks of success. Count each one.
- Provide opportunities for students to "belong" and to feel special in some way.
- Challenge students so that learning must occur—boredom invites problems.
- Encourage students to contribute in and out of the classroom. They should be willing to ask for help from other students, which will give them more involvement in various activities.
- Give directions—don't assume they see the obvious.
- Allow students time after a confrontation to cool down and gain control of themselves.
- Remember that the student's anger is with himself. You're just the outlet.
- Offer choices during a confrontation and continue with the lesson.
- Avoid a "public show" in which teacher and student need to prove a win.
- Have high expectations so that excellence and appropriateness are the norm.

- Have positive expectations to get rid of at-risk student stereotypes.
- Catch students doing right often and make note of it.
- Avoid coming up with quick answers or solutions. Say "I need time. See me at... ."
- Allow students ownership of their problems, behaviors, and consequences.
- Accept mistakes and remember that we all make poor decisions sometimes.
- Alternative discipline practices are hard work but very effective.
- Humor is needed and works with difficult students.
- Bring out the best in a student when you can. Nobody is difficult all the time.
- Students learn in different ways, so allow for alternative methods and hands-on work.
- Take time to explain the logic of a request rather than to simply demand it.
- Let your human side show. Getting tough isn't the answer. They've seen tougher.
- Learn feedback skills such as "I know you'll come up with a solution."
- Allow freedom within limits.
- Value what you preach.
- Practice "active" rather than "reactive" discipline.
- Encourage self-reliance.
- Form objectives to higher levels of learning (analysis, synthesis, evaluation).
- Encourage parents to work with schools in designing avenues for their child (pp. 104–107).

More research on at-risk students in music and the other arts is necessary. In conclusion, the authors of this book are compelled to emphasize the need for additional (and continued) research. As funding for education continues to decline, more and more students are denied opportunities for arts experiences. It is tragic to deprive any child of the arts, but depriving at-risk students of arts experiences can lead to irreversible damage. There is much anecdotal evidence that suggests that music and the other arts are beneficial for students. It seems that these benefits may be even greater for at-risk students—many teachers report dramatic increases in student motivation as well as academic achievement. In most cases, however, the methods used to reach these conclusions tend to be more intuitive than empirical. While these types of teacher observations and insights are valuable, they do not provide the type of hard evidence that is required to warrant changes in educational policy. If we are to convince political leaders and school administrators of the inherent values of music and the other arts in the curriculum, if we are to ensure that all students will have access to the arts, we must arm ourselves with an arsenal of solid research studies.

Summary

Clearly, the role of the teacher in research is crucial. Teachers have the benefit of insight gained through daily interactions with students at risk. This "real-world" experience is a valuable resource for planning and conducting research that can yield helpful strategies for at-risk intervention. Music teachers, in collaboration with other education professionals, are in a unique position to conduct meaningful research, and much research still needs to be done. It is only through long-term, collaborative efforts among teachers, administrators, parents, community leaders, and professionals in related fields (such as psychology, education research, and so on) that the phenomenon we call "students at risk" can be lessened—and perhaps eradicated.

An Annotated Bibliography of References

Including the At-Risk Phenomenon, Dropout Prevention, and the Arts

References cited in the text are marked with an asterisk. References without an asterisk are not cited in the text, but they are listed because they can be useful to music educators who want to know more about at-risk and dropout problems. All the latter references are annotated; some of the references with asterisks are also annotated.

Acer, C. C. (1987). Crime, curriculum and the performing arts: A challenge for inner-city schools to consider integrated language, music, drama and dance experiences, a compensatory curriculum for at-risk urban minorities in elementary school. (Doctoral dissertation, State University of New York at Buffalo, 1987). *Dissertation Abstracts International, 48,* 3047.

> This study investigated the possibility that an integrated humanities program might reduce academic failure and juvenile delinquency and addresses priorities of curriculum planning and early childhood education. An extensive review of the literature is included.

Ackerman, D., & Perkins, D. N. (1989). Integrating thinking and learning across the curriculum. In H. H. Jacobs (Ed.), *Interdisciplinary curriculum: Design and implementation* (pp.15–18). Alexandria, VA: Association for Supervision and Curriculum in Development.

The importance of an integrated curriculum (including the fine and performing arts) for optimal thinking and learning is discussed.

Aldrich, K. R. (1989). Rhythm, movement and synchrony: Effective teaching tools. *Journal of Physical Education, Recreation, and Dance,* April, 91–94.

Arts integration using dance to improve self-esteem and research connecting movement to cognition is advocated.

*Allen, C. F., & Portis, J. (1992). *The comeback kid: The life and career of Bill Clinton.* New York: Birch Lane Press Books.

*Allen, J. O. (1991). Defusing the angry student—Specific suggestions to use with difficult students. In R. C. Morris & N. Schultz (Eds.), *A resource guide for working with youth at risk, vol. III* (pp. 104–107). Lancaster, PA: Technomic Publishing Company, Inc.

Allen provides excellent suggestions for dealing with difficult and/or hostile students in a productive manner.

*Altieri, D. (1991). At-risk students: Consider integrated strategies. *Education Canada, 3* (13), 24–26.

Early intervention, teacher empowerment, parental involvement, and community involvement are advised.

Americans and the arts VI: Highlights from a nationwide survey of public opinion. (1992). New York: American Council for the Arts, 1 East 53rd Street, New York, NY 10022-4201.

Anderson, S. M. (1975). *The dropout prevention program, 1971–72 regular and 1972 summer school terms: Consolidated program information report.* National Center for Education Statistics (DHEW), Washington, D.C.

The data in this report are from the 1972 Consolidated Program Information Report (CPIR). The report is designed to provide statistical information about federal educational aid programs at the local level. These data focus on the characteristics of the children who participated, the total staff involved, and all expenditures incurred in the operation of federal dropout programs in local school districts.

Austin, J. R. (1990). The relationship of music self-esteem to degree of participation in school and out-of-school music activities among upper-elementary students. *Contributions to Music Education, 17,* 20–31.

Self-Esteem of Music Ability Scale (SEMA) and demographic data of grade, sex, participation in school music activities, and participation in out-of-school music activities were examined. Regression analysis indicated that self-esteem accounted for approximately 18% of the variance in school music participation and 17% of the variance in out-of-school music participation.

Baker, W. P., & Jensen, C. (1973). Mexican American, black, and other graduates and dropouts: A follow-up study covering 15 years of change, 1956–1971, fourth in a five-year series of follow-up studies of school leavers of the East Side Union High School District (p. 1). San Jose, CA: East Side Union High School District.

This report was the fourth in a series of follow-up studies conducted every five years by the East Side Union High School District. The purpose of the report was to assist the district in assessing organization, curriculum, and guidance services in "the light of ethnically analyzed responses."

*Barry, N. H. (1995). Forging a school/university partnership to promote arts education. Unpublished manuscript. (Additional information available from the author at 5040 Haley Center, Auburn University, AL 36849-5212.)

This partnership began as an informal arrangement to provide arts experiences for students in Lee County (a rural Alabama school system) and to provide opportunities for field experiences for Auburn University students enrolled in arts education courses. As trust and interest increased, the partnership evolved into a more formal and comprehensive arrangement. An Alabama State Council on the Arts Special Projects Grant was used to conduct a needs assessment, to fund a team visit to observe outstanding arts programs, and to fund special training in Discipline-Based Arts Education for Lee County teachers. The school system continues to seek ways to provide arts experiences for all students. Applications for additional grant funding have been submitted.

*Barry, N. H. (1996). Integrating the arts into the curriculum. *General Music Today, 9* (2), 9–13.

This article describes ways that music specialists and classroom teachers can work together to develop an integrated curriculum. Examples of lessons and learning activities are included.

*Barry, N. H. (1992). Project ARISE: Meeting the needs of disadvantaged students through the arts. *The Professional Educator, XIV* (2), 1–7.

Project ARISE (Arts Restoring and Increasing Self-Esteem) provided experiences in dance, dramatics, music and visual arts for underprivileged children. Comparison of children's self-concept scores from before and after participation in the project indicated significant improvements in self-esteem.

*Barry, N. H., Taylor, J. A., & Walls, K.C. (1990). *The role of the fine and performing arts in high school dropout prevention.* Tallahassee, FL: Center for Music Research.

This report indicates that arts programs provide a supportive, nourishing environment for students who border on dropping out of school. In many cases, at-risk students remain in school solely because of their interest in and commitment to band, chorus, orchestra, dance, drama, painting, sculpture, or other arts programs.

*Bartocci, B. (1992, August 11). Children of triumph. *Woman's Day,* pp. 32–34.

The author narrates four stories of handicapped or at-risk children who found success through the arts and other activities.

*Bass, A. (1991). Promising strategies for at-risk youth. *ERIC Digest, 59.* Eugene, OR: ERIC Clearinghouse on Educational Management (ERIC Document Reproduction Service No. ED 328958).

This article stresses the importance of intervention, parental involvement, the individual student, attainable student goals, and smaller classes and schools. Three successful school-based dropout programs are described.

Beaulieu, L. J. (Ed.) (1989). *Building partnerships for people: Addressing the rural south's human capital needs* (SRDC No. 117). Mississippi State, MS: Southern Rural Development Center.

Beaulieu documents the prevalence of illiteracy and dropouts in the South and its effect on unemployment. References include the influence of parents' values on aspirations and how to improve rural schools.

Blackler, R. (1970). *Fifteen plus: School leavers and the outside world.* London: George Allen & Unwin, Ltd.

The Avondale Project was one of the first attempts to bridge the gap between school and work for fifteen-year-old school leavers in England. Music was an important tool for reaching many at-risk students involved in this project.

Blum, D. L., & Jones, L. A. (1993). Academic growth group and mentoring program for potential dropouts. *School Counselor, 40* (3), 207–217.

Focuses on what can be done in intermediate or middle school to identify potential dropouts and conduct effective counselor groups and mentoring programs to keep these high risk students in school. Describes programs designed to provide potential dropouts with a support system that helps them develop positive attitudes about themselves, resulting in improved academic achievement. Relevant forms are appended.

*Bond, C. L., Smith, L. J., Ross, S. M., Nunnery, J. A., & Goldstein, R. R. (1992). *An alternative for teaching "at risk" children? A look at sing, spell, read, and write* (Policy/Practice Brief No. 9302.) Memphis, TN: Memphis State University, Center for Research in Educational Policy.

The Sing, Spell, Read, and Write (SSRW) Program teaches children in grades K–3 to spell, read, and write words by singing and listening to songs that incorporate the sounds of letters and letter combinations. The program was initiated in 1988 (11 schools in Memphis), and this article is a report of an evaluation of SSWR. The effectiveness of the program was dependent upon type of task, grade level, and socioeconomic strata. Generally, SSRW was found more effective for younger children (kindergarten and first grade) and for children of low economic status—many of them at risk.

Booth, David. (1985). "Imaginary gardens with real toads": Reading and drama in education. *Theory-into-Practice, 24* (3), 193–98.

Reading and drama are closely related in the learning process, interacting to develop the same personal resources in the child and building links between print and experience, drama and reality, self and other. The pressure and authenticity of the drama can help children create new knowledge and make different and necessary connections.

Bowker, Ardy. (1992, May). The American Indian female dropout. *Journal of American Indian Education, 31,* 3–20.

The most important factor related to American Indian females staying in school is a caring adult during the adolescent years.

Bowman, P. H. and Matthews, C. V. (1960). *Motivations of youth for leaving school* (Cooperative Research Program #200). Quincy, IL: University of Chicago Quincy Youth Development Program.

This longitudinal investigation asked dropouts and stayins about their junior high activities including music, art, and drama. Dropouts had fewer extracurricular activities than stayins.

*Brodinsky, B. & Keough, K. (1989). *Students at risk: Problems and solutions.* Arlington, VA: American Association of School Administrators.

This is a comprehensive study of the at-risk problem. The scope of the problem, identification of its various elements, and proposed solutions are addressed.

Brooks, B. K. (1989). A comparison of the characteristics and perceptions of Hispanic female high school dropouts and persisters. *Dissertation Abstracts International, 51,* 128A.

This study found that Hispanic female persisters participate in extracurricular activities more often than dropouts.

*Broudy, H. S. (1988). *The uses of schooling.* New York: Routledge.

*Bruner, J. S. (1960). *The process of education.* Cambridge, MA: Harvard University Press.

Bucci, J. A., & Reitzammer, A. F. (1992, Fall). Teachers make the critical difference in dropout prevention. *The Educational Forum, 57,* 63–70.

Includes a description of practical ways teachers can help at-risk students.

Burgard, R. (1989). The A+ program—The arts and academic excellence. In *Proceedings of the Symposium on the Importance of Music in Education* (pp. 46–54). Duxbury, MA: South Shore Conservatory.

This report describes programs using arts in the curriculum including the Ashley River Creative Arts School in Charleston, South Carolina, which in turn was inspired by the Elm Elementary School in Milwaukee. Ashley River now has the second highest academic rating in the city of Charleston.

Byerly, C. L. (1967). A school curriculum for prevention and remediation of deviancy. In D. Schreiber (Ed.), *Profile of the school dropout.* New York: Vintage Books.

Byerly explains the importance of involving "problem" students in all aspects of the school environment. Frequently, in such subject areas as art and music, a child achieves a sense of identity that carries over into his or her other classes.

Callaway, R. (1987). *Adolescent's "meaning" of leisure.* (ERIC Document Reproduction Service No. ED 292959).

This study examined the attitudes of 85 high school students toward various leisure activities. A variety of activities were rated on four scales. Attending music events, travel, and socializing were considered "high-class."

*Center for the Arts in the Basic Curriculum, Inc. Located at 58 Fearing Road, Hingham, MA 02043.

CABC is a nonprofit group assisting educational improvement and the community through the arts.

*Center for Disease Control (1993). *Teen gun deaths hit new high* [On-line]. Available: cyfcec@staff.tc.umn.edu.

*Cheshire, H. R. (1991). Project success. In R. C. Morris & N. Schultz (Eds.), *A resource guide for working with youth at risk, II* (pp. 24–27). Lancaster, PA: Technomic Publishing Company, Inc.

A successful intervention program for at-risk students is described.

Ciborowski, J. (1986). An examination of interests among achieving and underachieving adolescents (Doctoral dissertation, Claremont Graduate School, 1986). *Dissertation Abstracts International, 47,* 497.

This study dealt with the interests of achieving and underachieving high school students. Achieving students showed significantly more interest than underachieving students in life activities that involved music, drama, individual needs and comforts, and persons of their own sex.

*Coleman, H. L. K. (1995, January). Cultural factors and the counseling process: Implications for school counselors. *The School Counselor, 42,* 180–210.

> This article describes a club that was developed to provide minority students with a distinct peer reference group that promoted academic achievement: The Scholar's Club. The author concludes that "student self-esteem is bolstered through successful experiences when those experiences are valued by their peer culture in the immediate community for which they get positive feedback and recognition."

Collett, M. J. (1991). Read between the lines: Music as a basis for learning. *Music Educators Journal, 78* (3), 42–45.

> The Learning to Read through the Arts program, a collaborative effort by arts specialists, reading specialists, and classroom teachers requires one hour minimum of separate music instruction. It has been used in grades K–12 and with bilingual and special ed. students.

*Comer, J. (1984). *Improving American education: Roles for parents.* (Hearing before the Select Committee on Children, Youth and Families, June 7, 1984, pp. 55–60) Washington, DC: Remediation and Training Institute.

> The Comer Process integrated the teaching of basic skills with the teaching of mainstream (middle-class) arts and social skills.

Conley, D. (1993). A S. M. A. R. T. approach to helping at-risk students. *American Secondary Education, 22* (1), 23–25.

> The Sophomore Mentoring At-Risk Tracking Program (S. M. A. R. T.) is an invention program for at-risk students at a large high school. Students were invited to join the special class (met daily for one hour), with the permission of their parents and the signing of an attendance contract. Both the school psychologist and a teacher specialist taught the class, which involved

talks about social behavior, how to improve self-esteem, improving attendance, how to solve conflicts with teachers and peers, etc.). Feedback from the community, teachers, and administrators was very positive, and the program seems to have met its goal of reducing dropouts at the sophomore level.

*Conrath, J. (1989, August). Dropout prevention: Find out if your program passes or fails. *Executive Educator, 10* (8), 15–16.

Designed to help administrators answer important questions about student needs and dropout program effectiveness, this article provides a basic checklist of recommended characteristics, including a cohesive, systemwide strategy, clearly identified at-risk students, well-clarified roles, caring attitudes toward students, tough and compassionate staff, and other features.

Conrath, J. (1988, January). Time for action: A new deal for at-risk students. *NASSP Bulletin 72* (504), 36–40.

Although schools can do little to help youth from desperately poor, violent, or drug-addicted families, they can educate other at-risk youngsters who are discouraged or defeated learners. Schools can raise these students' self-esteem by bestowing serious work assignments instead of "warm fuzzies," solitary learning space, or external rewards for everyday accomplishments.

Cooper, D. H. & Speece, D. L. (1988). A novel methodology for the study of children at risk for school failure. *The Journal of Special Education 22* (2), 186–198.

This article presents the conceptual design of a three-year investigation of first-grade children at risk for school failure and illustrates the potential of a novel methodology for understanding the contribution of child characteristics and learning environments to the development of a child's status as at risk.

Costello, L. (Ed.). (1995). *Part of the Solution: Creative alternatives for youth.* Washington, DC: National Assembly of State Arts Agencies.

The purpose of this attractive publication is "to share some of these stories that illustrate the positive difference made in the lives of children and their families by artists, arts organizations, and community groups with assistance from the National Endowment for the Arts, the 56 state and jurisdictional arts agencies, and the seven regional arts organizations" (from the Foreword, n.p.). Arts projects in the various arts are cited in 11 states: Arizona, Maryland, Vermont, California, Louisiana, South Carolina, Colorado, Rhode Island, Oregon, Texas, and Virginia. This book concludes with short narratives of 52 additional projects throughout the country. This is a highly recommended publication and may be obtained from the National Assembly of State Arts Agencies, 1010 Vermont Avenue, Suite 920, Washington, DC, 20005, 202-347-6352.

Crawford, J. G. (1987). The school dropout: A case study of individual school dropouts which identifies the "at risk" variables which contribute to the development of a profile of the early school leaver (Doctoral dissertation, Iowa State University, 1986). *Dissertation Abstracts International, 47,* 4324A.

This study identifies factors that may place a student at risk with regard to successfully completing high school and receiving a diploma. Individual variables do not act in isolation to either "prevent" or "cause" a student to drop out of school. In most cases singular "at risk" variables began to accumulate prior to the student's enrolling in school. The final outcome of this pattern of failure is the student deciding to drop out of school.

*Crutsinger, C. (1991). Diamonds for teens. In R. C. Morris & N. Schultz (Eds.), *A resource guide for working with youth at risk, vol. II* (pp. 29–32). Lancaster, PA: Technomic Publishing Company, Inc.

The "Diamonds for Teens" program trains students to work with their at-risk peers. It involves the "Brainworks Questioning Model for Social and Emotional Growth" as the focal point of the program. "Brainworks" consists of five hierarchical levels of questioning ranging from general inquiry to summary and concluding statement, with each level requiring a more complex and abstract skill. A description of Brainworks is available from Carla Crutsinger, Brainworks, Inc., 1918 Walnut Plaza, Carrollton, TX 75006.

*Csikszentmihalyi, M. (1990). *Flow: The psychology of optimal experience*. New York: Harper & Row.

Cullen, C., & Moed, M. G. (1988). Serving high-risk adolescents. *New Directions for Community Colleges, 63,* 37–49.

Characteristics of a high-risk population are described. Successful programs emphasize project outcomes, changing the role of student from passive receptor to student as worker, editor, writer, or producer.

Curley, J. R. (1991). Recently enacted programs to address the dropout problem in New York State. *Urban Review, 23* (3), 159–72.

Executive and legislative branches of the New York State government have made consistent efforts to address the dropout problem, which is particularly acute in urban schools, through new initiatives and increased funding. State aid programs are summarized, and suggestions for improvement are provided.

*Damico, S. B., & Roth, J. (1991). *The neglected dropout: General track students*. Paper presented at the Annual Meeting for the American Educational Research Association, Chicago, IL. (ERIC Document Reproduction Service No. ED 331176)

*Dapena, R., Gatti, E., & Nadal, V. T. (1991). The ESOL/Bilingual counselor in Montgomery County Public Schools, Rockville, MD: A "multidimensional role" (pp. 113–114). In R. C. Morris & N. Schultz (Eds.), *A resource guide for working with youth at risk, vol. II*. Lancaster, PA: Technomic Publishing Company, Inc.

Davidson, L. (1989). Models of learning in schools—The different ways that children learn. In *Proceedings of the Symposium on the Importance of Music in Education* (pp. 1–9). Duxbury, MA.: South Shore Conservatory.

Education must attend to the whole personality. The arts are uniquely suited to do this because personal expression is foremost.

*Davis, W., & McCaul, E. (1990). *At-risk children and youth: A crisis in our schools and society.* Augusta, ME: State Department of Educational and Cultural Services.

Summarizes and discusses major issues concerning contemporary definitions of "at risk," the history of concern over at-risk children, general factors and conditions involved in placing children at risk, and contemporary issues regarding this population.

Dayton, C. W., Raby, M., & Stern, D. S. (1992). The California Partnership Academies: Remembering the "forgotten half." *Phi Delta Kappan, 73* (8), 539–545.

A description of vocational education for the at-risk student.

*Dean, J., & Gross, I. L. (1992). Teaching basic skills through arts and music. *Phi Delta Kappan, 73* (8), 613–616, 618.

LEAP (Learning through an Expanded Arts Program) demonstrates that the stimulation and involvement generated by hands-on experience with art and music can help students learn academic subjects.

*Deaton, C. D., & Blair, J. (1991). School initiatives that make a difference. In R. C. Morris & N. Schultz (Eds.), *A resource guide for working with youth at risk, vol. II* (pp. 158–161). Lancaster, PA: Technomic Publishing Company, Inc.

An integrated program with a strong hands-on component including arts and crafts is presented.

Dehyle, D. (1992, January). Constructing failure and maintaining cultural identity: Navajo and Ute school leavers. *Journal of American Indian Education, 3,* 24–47.

An ethnographic study indicating how the school and community social and political atmosphere contributed to students' decisions to drop out of school.

Developing work-study programs for potential dropouts: A manual. (1971). Albany, New York.: University of the State of New York, The State Education Department Bureau of Guidance.

> "This report is the fourth in a series of follow-up studies conducted every five years by the East Side [New York] Union High School District" (p. 1). Questionnaires were mailed to 2448 graduates and 1286 dropouts. A number of statistics are reported, including the fact that graduates had more participation in all activities and services than dropouts and that graduates placed more value on the activities than did the dropouts. It was recommended that "an increased emphasis on education for leisure and participation in community affairs should be given in art, music... ." (p. 10).

*Diem, R. A. (1991). *Dealing with the tip of the iceberg: School responses to at-risk behaviors.* Paper presented at the Annual Meeting of the American Educational Research Association, Chicago, IL. (ERIC Document Reproduction Service No. ED 333080).

> Case studies of 28 at-risk black, white, and Hispanic secondary students and the outcomes of their school-based intervention programs are presented. Common risk activities are observed and results of the study are described in terms of the complexity of the problems, the frustrations involved, satisfaction of these students' needs, the effectiveness of long-term behavioral changes, and other topics.

*Doran, E. (1992). What is a kid? In *Of kids, toys, choices, and such.* San Antonio, TX: Trevino Pub. Co.

Doss, David A. (1986). *Ninth-grade course enrollment and dropping out.* Paper presented at the 67th Annual Meeting of the American Educational Research Association, San Francisco, CA, April 16–20.

> This informal study examined the types of courses taken by at-risk ninth-grade high school students (aca-

demic years 1978–79 to 1982–83) in the Austin, Texas, Independent School District who later dropped out of school. Classes with above-average "holding power" included Spanish, introductory algebra, world history, dance, photography, biology, drawing and painting, and varsity sports. Band students remained higher at risk than those who participated in varsity sports, but the investigators state that due to the informal nature of the study, conclusions should be drawn cautiously.

*Dougherty, J. W. (1990). *Effective programs for at-risk adolescents* (Phi Delta Kappa Fastback 308). Bloomington, IN: Phi Delta Kappa Educational Foundation.

Dougherty provides a concise overview of at-risk characteristics and outlines examples of successful intervention programs. Brief and informative, this publication provides an excellent introduction to some of the important issues.

Dropouts, pushouts, and other casualties (1989). Bloomington, IN: Phi Delta Kappa, Center on Evaluation, Development, and Research.

This publication defines the dropout problem and reviews national data on the topic. It also correlates dropping out of school with reading achievement and other variables, and proposes a dropout intervention program (an evaluation design is included). Finally, some school reforms relative to at-risk students are described.

Dropout prevention: A manual for developing comprehensive plans. (1986). Tallahassee, FL: Department of Education, Division of Public Schools, Bureau of Compensatory Education and the University of Miami, FL: College of Education and Allied Professions, Florida Center for Dropout Prevention.

This report provides criteria for early identification of potential dropouts.

Dropout prevention: First report of program effectiveness for the 1987–1988 school year. (1989). Tallahassee, FL: Department of Education Division of Public Schools, Bureau of Compensatory Education Dropout Prevention Section.

> The goal of the Dropout Prevention Act of 1986 was to restructure, expand, and enhance the alternative education programs in the State. This act identified five programmatic categories: educational alternatives, teenage parents, substance abuse, disciplinary, and youth services programs. It includes requirements for dropout retrieval. Dropout prevention programs authorized by the Dropout Prevention Act of 1986 also are described. Strategies used to achieve the program objectives included small classes with an average teacher/pupil ratio of 1:15; teaching to students' learning styles; experiential learning (hands-on); community service; course modifications, more frequent and intensive counseling; alternate means of assessment, peer tutoring; and cooperative learning.

Duerksen, G. L., & Darrow, A. (1991). Music class for the at-risk: A music therapist's perspective. *Music Educators Journal, 78* (3), 46–49.

> Extracurricular activities may increase the attractiveness of the school. Music classes may allow the students to practice self-discipline, especially highly structured large ensembles. Music can unify students and increase self-esteem.

*Dryfoos, J. G. (1990). *Adolescents at risk: Prevalence and prevention.* New York: Oxford University Press.

> Dryfoos presents a comprehensive review of research literature in delinquency, substance abuse, teen pregnancy, and school failure as well as the elements of prevention programs that change specific behaviors. The review was sponsored by the Carnegie Corporation for the project "Adolescents-at-Risk: A Strategy for Intervention." The author defines "at risk" as "children who are at high risk of never becoming responsible adults." The book contains many references and statistics.

*Eisner, E. (1985). Aesthetic modes of knowing. In Eisner, E.

(Ed.), *Learning and teaching: The ways of knowing, Part II* (pp. 23–36). Chicago: The University of Chicago Press.

*Eisner, E. W. (1992). The misunderstood role of the arts in human development. *Phi Delta Kappan,* 591–595.

*Ensley, S., McGuire, K., Moose, B., & Everett, P. (1991). Parents: A necessary link. In R. C. Morris & N. Schultz (Eds.), *A resource guide for working with youth at risk, vol. II* (pp. 221–222). Lancaster, PA: Technomic Publishing Company, Inc.

> Strategies employed by the Union County Middle School to promote parental involvement included personal invitations to open house at the school, in-home visitations, sharing family crises, regular written communication with parents, open home telephone policy, and scheduled personal conferences at the parents' convenience.

Fowler, C. (1989). Music education develops the skills the business community requires. In *Proceedings of the Symposium on the Importance of Music in Education* (pp. 20–27). Duxbury, MA: South Shore Conservatory.

> The arts connect with the larger educational agenda. Fowler suggests five areas where the arts can make natural and unique connections with the deeper purposes of education. All relate directly to mentation in every art form, and at the same time develop abilities that are generally not being taught as well as other subjects.

*Franklin, C. & Streeter, C. L. (1995). Assessment of middle class youth at-risk to dropout: School, psychological and family correlates. *Children and Youth Services Review, 17* (3), 433–48.

Frymier, J. (1992). *Growing up is risky business, and schools are not to blame* (Final report: Phi Delta Kappa study of students at risk, viols. I & II). Bloomington, Indiana: Phi Delta Kappa.

> An excellent resource, these volumes present the final report from an extensive study. Volume I describes in

narrative form how Phi Delta Kappa came to study students at risk and interprets the data. Volume II describes attempts to validate a scale to predict risk among young people and presents data collected from 21,706 students.

Funk, S. (1991). Music makes the difference. *PMEA News, 55* (4), 4.

PMEA News is the official publication of the Pennsylvania Music Educators Association. This article is a narrative of a young at-risk student who "discovered" music (chorus and cello). He worked diligently at music, became a good performer, and gained self-esteem that transferred to his other classes.

Gads, E. M., Hurlburt, G., & Fuqua, D. R. (1992). The use of the self-directed search to identify American Indian high school dropouts. *The School Counselor, 39,* 311–315.

Among American Indian students in this study, those with Realistic personality types (preferring manual occupations) were most likely to drop out.

Gainer, W. J. (1986). *Statement of William J. Gainer, Associate Director of Human Resources Division, before the Subcommittee on Elementary, Secondary, and Vocational Education, House Committee on Education and Labor, on the school dropout problem* (GAO Publication No. 129915). Washington, DC: U. S. General Accounting Office.

Gainer, W. J. (1986). *School dropouts: The extent and nature of the problem* (GAO Publication No. B-223294). Washington, DC: U. S. General Accounting Office.

Ganley, Natalie (1983). Learning to read through the arts. *Design for Arts in Education, 84,* 11–13.

Reading-Oriented Arts Workshops, held for students from 9–14 years of age (when they are most receptive to the arts), had the arts at the core of the curriculum. Students kept journals of their instruction in and participation in the arts.

*Gardner, H. (1985). *Frames of mind: The theory of multiple intelligences.* New York, NY: Basic Books.

> Gardner's research has identified seven intelligences (i.e., distinct ways that people learn and know) including verbal/linguistic, logical/mathematical, visual/spatial, body/kinesthetic, musical/rhythmic, interpersonal, and intrapersonal intelligence.

*Garibaldi, A.M., & Bartley, M. (1987). Black school pushouts and dropouts: Strategies for reduction. *The Urban League Review, 11,* 227–235.

> This report provides data about attendance rates, disciplinary problems, and other factors associated with students at risk. Proactive strategies are recommended. The importance of providing creative arts experiences is pointed out.

*Garrett, M. W. (1995). Between two worlds: Cultural discontinuity in the dropout of native American youth. *School Counselor, 42* (3), 186–95.

*Giamatti, A. B. (1981). New York: Athenum.

Gilbert, M. B. (1982). *An enrichment program for migrant students: MENTE/UOP.* Paper presented at the Council for Exceptional Children Conference on the Bilingual Exceptional Child, Phoenix, AZ. (ERIC Document Reproduction Service No. ED 234536)

> The report describes a summer enrichment program— Migrantes Envueltos en Nuevos Temas de Educacion/Migrant—for promising and talented migrant high schoolers. Program offering focused on language arts, quantitative skills, theatre arts, fine arts, physical development, personal development, and recreation. Arts courses included introduction to arts (appreciation and practical), music appreciation, theatre, singing, dance, drama, and other expressive culturally based performing arts emphasizing growth of self-esteem.

Giles, M. M. (1990). *An investigation of effective styles of music to alter mood in first and second graders at risk for construct disorders in a classroom environment: Application of the vectoring effect.* Paper presented to the Virginia Arts Leadership Conference, Williamsburg, VA.

> Giles's paper describes a study that investigated the effectiveness of three styles of music to alter mood in first and second graders who showed early signs of aggressive behavior (and thus could be considered at risk). She found that electronic music and Disney movie music were more effective in altering mood than classical music.

Glaser, R. E. (1982). *Keeping high risk students in school.* Paper presented at the 66th annual meeting of the National Association of Secondary School Principals, San Francisco, CA.

> Ohio's Occupational Work Adjustment (OWA) program was a one- to two-year ungraded vocational program for 14- and 15-year-olds who have been identified as potential dropouts from the regular educational program. This report also includes a review of the literature on the dropout problem.

*Glasser, W. (1969). *Schools without failure.* New York: Harper & Row.

*Godfrey, R. (1992). Civilization, education, and the visual arts: A personal manifesto. *Phi Delta Kappan,* 596–598, 600.

> Godfrey contends that to continually cheat on art is to deny the potential of human achievement.

Goldberg, M. R. (1992). Expressing and assessing understanding through the arts. *Phi Delta Kappan,* 619–623.

> Goldberg explores the potential of using arts activities to access student learning.

Goldsmith, Robert G. (1987). *Students concerned about tomorrow: A dropout intervention program* (final report). Abington, VA: People, Inc.

In this successful program, two of the classes planned and produced their own video show.

Goodlad, J. I., & Morrison, J. (1981, Jan/Feb). The arts in education. *Design,* 15-2.

Goodlad and Morrison present a powerful argument for the value of arts in education.

Gorby, J. (1993, Winter). Support for school music and the other arts. *The Sinfonian, 41* (1), 4–7.

The author describes two recent events that "should inspire all arts educators, parents, and everyone who believes in the future of our children through the rightful place of the arts as basic in education." One is the partnership of the U.S. Department of Education and the National Endowment of the Arts; the other is the results of a poll conducted by the American Music Conference that measured adults' attitudes toward music. The results of the poll show that parents consider music essential for their children and for themselves.

*Gordon, D. A. (1993). The current status and future implications of obtaining follow-up data from graduates of specialized schools of the arts in the United States. (Doctoral dissertation, Florida State University, 1993). *Dissertation Abstracts International, 54,* 07A.

Gottfredson, G. D., et al. (1983). *The school action effectiveness study plus second interim report, part II* (Report No. 342). Baltimore, MD: Johns Hopkins University, Center for Social Organization of Schools.

This report includes results of 14 specific programs including the Jazzmobile Alternative Arts Education Project, which involved juveniles in the sixth through eighth grades who exhibited disruptive behavior, were chronic absentees and truants, or had experienced academic failure. The students had daily classes in drama, music, dance, or visual arts in classes of less than 10. The instructors were caring and related culturally to the students, encouraging valuing of school by teaching discipline through the arts. The evaluation of the program was not planned, so little effect was empirically measured, although participants claimed success.

*Green, P. C. D., & Berry, N. S. (1992). Songs for at-risk students. *D. C. Music Educator, 26* (3), 10–11.

*Gregorc, A. (1985). *Inside styles: Beyond the basics.* Columbia, CT: Gregorc Associates.

This book discusses learning styles and the importance of addressing individual differences in the classroom.

*Gregory, S. S. (1992). The hidden hurdle. *Time* (March 16), 44–46.

Talented black students find that one of the most insidious obstacles to achievement comes from a surprising source: their own peers. Interviews with students, parents, and educators point out that black students may feel compelled to sabotage their own learning to fit in with their peers.

*Grossnickle, Donald R. (1986). *High school dropouts: Causes, consequences, and cure.* (Phi Delta Kappa Fastback #242). Bloomington, IN: Phi Delta Kappa Educational Foundation.

This useful booklet cites early-warning signs for students at risk of dropping out. Grossnickle goes on to point out that each case is individual and requires a thorough investigation. Several individual case studies complete the report.

Growing up complete: The imperative for music education. (1991). Reston, VA: Music Educators National Conference.

This is an excellent resource for music educators. The document is available from MENC. Contact Publication Sales, 1806 Robert Fulton Drive, Reston, VA 20191-4348; phone: 800-336-3768 or 703-860-4000.

*Gudeman, J. A. (1987). High school dropouts: A study of preventive strategies (Doctoral dissertation, Saint Louis

University, 1987). *Dissertation Abstracts International, 48,* 789A.

> This study focused on the causes of high school dropouts. The author states that high school dropouts can be prevented with far less effort and expense when preventive strategies are implemented during the preschool years and the first few grades of elementary school.

*Hadley, W. H., & Hadley, R. T. (1991). Effective strategies for at-risk students. In R. C. Morris & N. Schultz (Eds.), *A resource guide for working with youth at risk, vol. II* (pp. 53–55). Lancaster, PA: Technomic Publishing Company, Inc.

> Music and its role in motivating students to develop skills in language arts, mathematics and social studies are described.

*Hanna, J. L. (1992). Connections: Arts, academics, and productive citizens. *Phi Delta Kappan, 73* (8), 601–607.

> A case for the relationship of arts education to achievement in other academic disciplines and the world of work is established.

Hansen, J. B., et al. (1986). *Elementary summer school, 1985 program in the Portland Public Schools.* Portland, OR: Department of Research, Evaluation, and Testing, Public Schools.

> Courses offered in the summer program included arts and crafts as well as basic and remedial instruction in reading, mathematics, and language. Results were examined for students who were not promoted, for remedial students, and for talented and gifted students. Most groups benefited the most in math. Students who were not promoted did less well that in the overall district in reading and language. Remedial students showed gains, compared to the district, especially in reading and mathematics.

Hanshumaker, J. (1986, Spring). The effects of music and other arts instruction on reading and math achievement and on general school performance. *Update: Applications of Research in Music Education,* 10–11.

> The author points out that although arts teachers value artistic goals, there has not been a tradition of support for them in the public schools. On the other hand, "there is a body of research that supports the case of the arts in public schools and does so in terms that relate to the common concerns expressed by public school personnel." Research findings are summarized, and a bibliography of studies from 1978 through 1985 is presented.

Hanson, J. R. (1989). *Learning styles, types of intelligence, and students at risk: An argument for a broad-based curriculum.* Moorestown, NJ: Hanson Silver Strong & Associates.

*Hanson, J. R. (1990, March). *Learning styles, types of intelligence and students at risk: Music education as a catalyst for needed change.* Paper presented at the Music Educators National Conference, Washington, DC.

> The at-risk student is an extroverted, sensing, feeling, and action-oriented type of learner whose learning style is often not accommodated in the curriculum. Hanson cites research supporting this idea and describes the four learning styles (sensing-feeling, sensing-thinking, intuitive-feeling, and intuitive-thinking) that when taken collectively, represent "psychic health or wholeness."

*Hanson, J. R., Silver, H. F., & Strong, R. W. (1991). Square pegs: Learning styles of at-risk students. *Music Educators Journal, 78* (3), 30–35.

> Hanson contends that music teachers are more likely than other teachers to learn and teach in a feeling style. Music and self-expression motivate at-risk students to learn. Involvement teaching is encouraged— students express feelings and passions, plan and execute their work.

Hayes, D. W. (1994). Higher standards: Tougher curriculum drives down dropouts. *Black Issues in Higher Education, 10,* 40–42.

The author reports that research by Mirel (Northern Illinois University) and Angus (University of Michigan) shows a decline in dropout rate between 1982 and 1990. The decline was from 18–14% for African American high school students but unchanged for Hispanic students (32%). The rise in minority students taking three years each of math and science was even more dramatic: from 10–41% of African American students and from 6–33% of Hispanic students. SAT scores for minorities also have risen; but it is disturbing to note that the number of African American students going to college is not growing at the same rate.

Healy, M. (1991, April 17). South Carolina school makes crafts part of the lesson plan. *USA Today,* 7.

The Ashley River Creative Arts Elementary School in Charleston, South Carolina, integrates the arts into all subjects. There is a waiting list of 1200 students, the school has 97% attendance, and 100% attendance at PTA meetings.

*Hershaff, S. M. (1978). Dropouts: Their general feelings of alienation and attitudes toward school compared to persisters (Doctoral dissertation, Rutgers University, 1978). *Dissertation Abstracts International, 39,* 2654A.

The purpose of this study was to identify differences in general feelings of alienation and in attitudes toward school dropouts and persisters. Significant results supported several conclusions about the relationship between student attitudes and dropping out of school.

*Hughes, W. O. (1992). Two programs for high-risk students. *General Music Today, 5* (2), 20.

Describes a multiarts program called "Studying the Environment through the Arts" and a semester-long general music course planned for a mainstreamed high school general music class.

Jahn, G. (1989, September 5). Creating harmony. *Tallahassee Democrat,* D1.

The article describes how the Harlem Boys Choir
affects participants in encouraging them to continue
their education. Tutoring is provided six days a week
as well at the choir's own school. All members must
maintain a B average. The members also travel over-
seas. Ninety-eight percent of Boys Choir members go
on to college, in contrast to 25% of New York blacks
that drop out of high school. The program serves 200
male and female students, ages 8–18.

*Jennings, L. (1988). New public awareness project aims to
focus on the high-risk young. *Education Week, 8 (14), 1, 20.*

Participants of the first High-Risk Youth Practicum
held at Yale University discussed many areas influencing the education of at-risk students, including poverty, physical abuse, and parental neglect. A public
awareness campaign, supported by the National
School Safety Center and the U.S. Office of Juvenile
Justice and Delinquency Prevention, has been planned
to go beyond the "Just Say No" campaign against
drugs sponsored by the White House. Families,
schools, and communities must be involved in teaching "pro-social" skills to high-risk youth. Statistics and
other research findings are cited to emphasize the
magnitude of the problem.

Johnson, C. D. (1985). Identifying potential school dropouts
(Doctoral dissertation, United States International University,
1984). *Dissertation Abstracts International, 45,* 2397A.

Variables that can be used to identify students who are
likely to drop out of high school prior to graduation
were identified. Results indicated that it is possible to
establish a set of reliable predictor variables consisting
of a combination of learning styles and historical student data that will identify students who might drop
out of school.

Johnson, J. L. (1985). A use of music to reduce discipline
problems in an inner-city junior high school (Doctoral dissertation, United States International University, 1985).
Dissertation Abstracts International, 46, 1861A.

This study investigated music as a process variable in

an effort to shed light on its function as a potential behavior modifier. Results showed that the presence of music but not the type of music affects the number of occurrences of inappropriate behaviors in a classroom. Students in classrooms where music was played as a background sound behaved better than those in class-rooms where no music was played.

*Johnson, R., & Barry, N. (1993, Fall/Winter). The arts and the at-risk child: A school and university partnership. *The School Community Journal,* 63–7.

A conference on arts and the at-risk child brought arts educators, school administrators, community leaders, and business representatives together to develop strategies for using community resources to provide arts experiences for at-risk children.

Jones, B. A. (1992). Collaboration: The case for indigenous community-based organization support of dropout prevention programming and implementation. *The Journal of Negro Education, 61,* 498–508.

Information about the effectiveness of school/nonprof-it collaboratives to reduce dropout rates.

Jones, D. (1991, April 17). Value of creative courses is hard to measure. *USA Today,* 7A.

When art was integrated into history at JFK High School in the Bronx, 68.7% of students passed a histo-ry standardized test, compared to 54% before. In a UCLA study, socioeconomically disadvantaged stu-dents' reading achievement score improved 13.2% after a 16-week program offering studio art. SAT scores for students that had 4.5 years of arts were sig-nificantly better than other students. In 1990, the aver-age verbal score was 424, but for arts students, it was 451; the average math score was 476, but for arts stu-dents, it was 496.

*Jurgens, D. A. (1985). Comparative analysis of characteristics of dropouts and persisters from a selected alternative sec-ondary school (Doctoral dissertation, University of Nebraska,

Lincoln, 1985). *Dissertation Abstracts International, 46,* 1463A.

> This study compared demographic, educational, fami-
> ly, personal, and occupational characteristics of persis-
> ters and dropouts in an alternative school.

Kardash, C. M., & Wright, L. (1987). Does creative drama benefit elementary school students: A meta-analysis. *Youth Theatre Journal, 1* (3), 193–98.

> The authors examined effects of creative drama on
> elementary school children's skills in four achieve-
> ment areas: reading, oral and written communication,
> person-perception, and drama skills. Results indicated
> that creative drama activities had a moderate, positive
> effect on children's performance across these achieve-
> ment areas.

*Keller, D., et. al. (1991). Total staff development: Do not begin dropout prevention without it. *Journal of School Leadership, 1* (4), 400–409.

> Effective, long-term dropout prevention will not occur
> without broad-based, in-depth, and ongoing staff
> development that changes educators' behavior toward
> at-risk students. Staff development planners should
> recognize that students respond not to programs but to
> individualized, personally delivered solutions and
> assistance promoting youngsters' self-acceptance.
> Community involvement is essential, because educat-
> ing everyone takes everyone in the community.

Kennedy, R. L. (1992). *Case study of a school phobic.* Paper presented at the Twenty-first Annual Meeting of the Mid-South Educational Research Association, Knoxville, TN.

> A student described as "not fitting the dropout picture"
> (i.e., white, middle-class, two-parent family) develops
> an intense hatred of public school resulting in absen-
> teeism and failure. Important factors in this problem
> include the "dehumanizing"effects of public school,
> the influence of peers, and rebellion against authoritar-
> ian control.

Kellmayer, J. (1993). Disruptive high-schoolers start over on the college campus. *Education Digest, 59,* 8–10.

> The author describes an alternative high school for disruptive and previously incarcerated students that is housed in a community college setting. Students take traditional high school courses, but "the critical component of the program's success is the complete immersion of the students in the college environment" (p. 9). Qualified students can take college courses, join college clubs, etc. The seven-year success rate is 80%, and many students continue on to college. Currently, there are seven county-wide alternative high schools on college campuses in New Jersey.

Koeller, S. (1989). School/community interaction. *Social Studies, 80* (1), 28–29.

> Teachers and community gained pride in students' writings because of high interest in students' artwork. Outstanding artwork was selected for purchase by merchants as ads in an elementary school's yearly literary magazine.

Koppenhaven, D. (1986, November 1). Effective programs combat adolescent illiteracy. *Common Focus, 7* (1), 2, 7.

> Based on preliminary observations from site visits to four literacy programs, the author indicates four common areas of strength found in all programs: "respect for teachers, administrators who facilitate success, students who know they are learning, and meaningful curricula that take into account the interests, needs, language, and experience of each student" (p. 7).

Kronish, M. & Abelmann, J. (1989). *Elementary: Focus on fine arts.* West Haven, CT: National Education Association Professional Library.

> This document offers an instructional framework and shows how an integrated approach can accommodate various learning styles. Case studies and classroom applications are presented to illustrate how the approach works. An integrated curriculum is motivating, it generates energy, it provides direction and

structure, and it activates the student's inner resources. This approach generates enthusiasm and excitement for teaching and learning.

*Lazear, D. G. (1991a). *Seven ways of knowing: Teaching for multiple intelligences.* Palatine, IL: Skylight Publishing.

Describes the Multiple Intelligence Theory from a teaching perspective. Provides exercises for developing different intelligences.

*Lazear, D. G. (1991b). *Seven ways of teaching: The artistry of teaching with multiple intelligences.* Palatine, IL: Skylight Publishing.

Lazear's useful discussion of "multiple intelligence theory" for teachers provides guides for lesson planning and many charts and graphs to facilitate implementation of Gardner's theories.

Lazear, D. G. (1992). *Teaching for multiple intelligences* (Phi Delta Kappa Fastback 342). Bloomington, IN: Phi Delta Kappa Educational Foundation.

The following research findings in intelligence are discussed: intelligence is not fixed or static, intelligence can be learned and taught, and intelligence is a multidimensional phenomenon that occurs at multiple levels of the brain/mind/body system. Music is one of these intelligences and occurs at all levels.

Learning to read through the arts evaluation report, 1981–86 (1987, April 20), and *Learning to read through the arts evaluation report, 1988–89.* (1990, May 5). Brooklyn NY: New York City Board of Education, Office of Research, Evaluation, and Assessment.

The Learning to Read through the Arts Program has been operating since 1971 under a Title I grant. It is an individualized reading and writing program designed to improve reading and writing skills through the integration of a total art program with total reading program. It has been expanded for use as a developmental and enrichment reading program for grades K–12, special education and bilingual students. The program builds self-confidence, improves self-image, and adds to the experiences of the participating children.

Leidig, L. R. A. (1983). A descriptive study of a successful inner-city high-school instrumental music program (Doctoral dissertation, University of Southern California, 1983). *Dissertation Abstracts International, 44,* 1370A.

This study describes a successful inner-city high school music program and attempts to account for such success, to discuss implications for teachers and potential teachers of inner-city high-school instrumental music programs, and to provide a basis for future field research.

Lerner, R. (1989). *"Not by bread alone": A report of the Southern Arts Federation.* Atlanta, GA: Southern Arts Federation.

The achievements and issues of and challenges for the arts in the South are expressed in this document. It is an outgrowth of the Southern Arts Federation's "Southern Arts Agenda" public meetings, which were held across the south in 1988 (involving a total of 1000 individuals). Five main topics are discussed (e.g., "What are the challenges the region is facing?"), along with four "related purposes" (e.g., "To describe, from the perspective of the arts, the regional environment which impacts on the arts, and support for the arts"). Order from the Southern Arts Federation, 1293 Peachtree Street, N.E., Suite 500, Atlanta, GA 30309; phone: 404-874-7244.

*Levin, H. M. (1987). *New schools for the disadvantaged.* Aurora, CO: Mid-Continent Regional Educational Laboratory. Costello, L. (Ed.). (1995).

School staffs should be empowered to make appropriate decisions and plans for at-risk intervention.

A lot to learn. (1990, Spring). Special issue, The world of children. *LIFE,* 57–59.

The Key School, a successful program based on the seven types of intelligence outlined by Howard Gardner, is described. Instruction in art and music are important parts of the curriculum at the Key School.

*Loken, J. O. (1973). *Student alienation and dissent.* Ontario: Prentice-Hall of Canada.

Alienated students have had difficulty relating their own experience to the experiences provided by the school. Some students cannot compete under conditions dictated by the school. Many talented students have been urged to keep up academically, when more effort should be spent on their attempting to become good writers, artists, sportsmen, or scientists in their own right.

*Lynn, L. (1992, November 29). El Paso teacher hits a smart note: Ex-drummer sings to teach English. *Austin American Statesman,* p. F2.

*MacRae-Campbell, L. (1991a). *The arts and the mind: Research supports arts education.* Seattle, WA: New Horizons for Learning.

The author lists five ways in which the arts can optimize teaching and learning, then provides research evidence. The five areas are integration of neurological functions, enhancing the learning environment, generating positive emotional responses to learning, accessing a variety of human intelligences, and engaging a variety of learning styles.

MacRae-Campbell, L. (1991b). Arts programs enhance student achievement. In *On the beam.* Seattle, WA: New Horizons for Learning.

Madsen, C. H., Jr., & Madsen, C. K. (1983). *Teaching/discipline: Behavioral principles toward a positive approach (3rd ed.).* Raleigh, NC: Contemporary Publishing, Inc.

The authors outline a behavioral approach to teaching with specific examples of applications and case studies. Observation techniques are discussed and examples of observation forms and other instruments are provided.

Maltester, J. (1986, January) Music—The social and academic edge. *THRUST (Association of California School Administrators)*, 25–27.

> Music teaches values, life outlook, and learning patterns.

*Marshall, A. T. H. (1978). An analysis of music curricula and its relationship to the self-image of urban black middle-school age children (Doctoral dissertation, The State University of New Jersey, 1977). *Dissertation Abstracts International, 38,* 6594A.

> The purpose of this study was to review published literature and previous research findings and to investigate the relationship between dimensions of the Black child's self-image and music education.

Martin, D. L. (1981). A study of the family, personal, and subjective characteristics of school dropouts in Kentucky (Doctoral dissertation, University of Kentucky, 1980). *Dissertation Abstracts International, 41,* 3357A.

> This study sought to (1) identify certain family, personal, and subjective characteristics that contribute to a student's dropping out of the Kentucky educational system, and (2) predict which students will leave school early. Of the 48 variables for which the null hypotheses were stated, 35 were found to be significantly related at the .05 level to the dependent variable dropout/persister.

Martorelli, D. (1992, October). The arts take center stage. *Instructor,* 38–39, 44–45.

> Martorelli provides a background report on the role of the arts as an essential component of elementary education.

McAnaney, H. (1990). *Computer-assisted instruction in teaching music literacy skills, music theory and application to severely emotionally disturbed children.* Paper presented at the Eighteenth Annual California Association of Private Special Education Schools conference, Timothy Murphy School, San Rafael, CA.

McAnaney describes his use of SongSmith software with emotionally disturbed children.

*McArthur, E. H. (1986). High school dropouts in Georgia (Doctoral dissertation, University of Georgia, 1986). *Dissertation Abstracts International, 47,* 1958A.

Results of this study generally supported the previous literature. Several findings, however, suggested changing trends: (1) No statistically significant differences were found between dropouts of higher and lower socioeconomic status in high school absentee rates or in student achievement, (2) Forces outside of school may have less influence on students of lower socioeconomic status to drop out than has previously been believed, (3) Evidence suggests that forces both in and out of school provide more encouragement for females to remain in school than for males, and (4) Evidence suggests that students who drop out have difficulty achieving their economic goals, and hence express a desire to return to school to complete their high school education.

McCarthy, K. (1980). The Guadalupe "Dropout School." *Momentum, 11,* 4–6.

What started as a summer arts and crafts program in the predominantly Mexican American Lower West Side of St. Paul, Minnesota, has developed into a "dropouts" school accepted into the public school system. The small school emphasizes strictness, caring, basic skills, and student responsibility.

*McCormick, K. (1989, January). *An equal chance: Educating at-risk children to succeed.* Alexandria, VA: National School Boards Association. (ERIC Document Reproduction Service No. ED 307359)

McLaughlin, J. (1990). *Building a case for arts education: An annotated bibliography of major research.* New York: American Council for the Arts.

*Means, B., & Knapp, M. S. (1991). Cognitive approaches to teaching advanced skills to educationally disadvantaged students. *Phi Delta Kappan,* 282–328.

*Mernit, S. (1992, October). Adding the arts. *Instructor,* 46.

> Despite financial constraints and a lack of arts
> resources, the Cleveland, Tennessee, School District
> has an outstanding arts-in-the-curriculum program.
> The Cleveland program demonstrates that "an exem-
> plary arts program doesn't require big spending, just
> big ideas." For more information, contact Jacquelynn
> Adams, Supervisor of Instruction, Cleveland City
> School System, 4300 Mouse Creek Road, Cleveland,
> TN 37312; phone: 615-472-9571.

*Meyer, L. H.; Harootunian, B.; William, D.; & Steinberg, A.
(1991). *Inclusive middle schooling practices: Shifting from
deficit to support models.* Paper presented at the Annual
Meeting of the American Educational Research Association,
Chicago, IL. (ERIC Document Reproduction Service No. ED
332355)

> The Syracuse Stay In School Partnership Project is
> described in this report. It was a collaborative project
> between Syracuse University and six district middle
> schools in New York (3200 children). All children
> were involved in the project, but at-risk students par-
> ticipated in two projects that were designed to lessen
> their feelings of alienation: cooperative learning and
> peer support networks.

*Middleton, R. W. (1980). The effectiveness of early identifi-
cation of potential high school dropouts (Doctoral dissertation,
Saint Louis University, 1979). *Dissertation Abstracts
International, 40,* 5677A.

> The profile of a dropout that developed in this study
> would indicate that the potential dropout would score
> slightly lower on IQ scores than would the graduate;
> would be perceived by the first grade teacher as lack-
> ing in social interaction skills; would progressively
> become a poorer reader as he or she passed through
> school; would score better on the nonverbal and math-
> ematic sections of tests rather than the verbal and lan-
> guage sections; and would exhibit a pattern of irregu-
> lar attendance.

*Mitchell, P., Lesser, H., & Strobias, L. (1988, January). I can be all of me. *Principal,* 19–22.

Washington's Fillmore Arts Center is a comprehensive
arts magnet school. More than 900 students from five
other schools are bused for a half day once a week.
They take four courses a year for a total of 68 hours of
arts instruction. The program demonstrates "that the
arts enhance physical, social, emotional, and cognitive
development, and that they introduce students to
skills, abilities, and inner resources that may otherwise
remain untapped."

*Modugno, A. D. (1991). The lost student found. *Music
Educators Journal, 78* (3), 50–54.

Case studies of at-risk students in an electronic music
class are presented.

Moritz, D. M. (1977). Socioeconomic and school-related factors as predictors of high school dropouts categorized by race
and sex (Doctoral dissertation, University of Kansas, 1977).
Dissertation Abstracts International, 38, 3857A.

Moritz found that it was possible to construct an equa-
tion that would predict dropouts for an unstratified
group. It was also found that greater accuracy of pre-
diction could be obtained through use of groups strati-
fied by race and sex.

*Morris, R. C., & Schultz, N. (Eds.) (1991). *A resource guide
for working with youth at risk, vol. II.* Lancaster, PA:
Technomic Publishing Company, Inc.

This volume contains abstracts of 90 papers from the
Second Southeastern Conference on Youth at Risk
(Savannah, GA, Feb. 14–16, 1991). They are orga-
nized into six sections: "Understanding Students At-
Risk," "Preventing and Reducing Incidence of At-
Risk," "Changing the System," "Strategies and
Programs for Working with At-Risk Youth," "Utilizing
Community Resources," and "Facilitating Parent
Involvement." Articles generally focus on strategies

that have been successful in actual practice. Copies may be purchased from Technomic Publishing Company, Inc., 851 New Holland Avenue, Box 3535, Lancaster, PA 17604.

Music Educators Journal, 78 (3), 1991 (November). Reston, VA: Music Educators National Conference.

An excellent resource, the entire issue is dedicated to the at-risk student: "Special Focus: Music and the At-Risk Student."

*Myles, O. (1984). Achievement scores and self-concept responses of eighth-grade potential and non-potential dropouts in the Mississippi school district. (Doctoral dissertation, University of Southern Mississippi, 1983). *Dissertation Abstracts International, 45,* 1260A.

Myles found that eighth-grade students identified as potential dropouts had significantly lower achievement test scores, but potential dropouts scored higher in four of five areas on the About Me Self-Concept report.

Nardini, M. L., & Antes, R. L. (1991). What strategies are effective with at-risk students? *NASSP Bulletin, 75* (538), 67–72.

A total of 178 secondary school principals at 100 schools were asked to evaluate the effectiveness of strategies used with at-risk youth. The most effective strategies were after-school programs, Chapter I programs, teacher aides, coping skills, and peer tutoring for middle schools; and individualized instruction, teacher aides, and summer school for high school students.

*National Committee for Prevention of Child Abuse (1993). *Teens and the hard facts* [On-line]. Available at: http://www.inetwave.com/stv.

*Niebur, L. (1992). Of gifts, needs, and Choctaw chiefs. *General Music Today, 5* (2), 8–9.

Niebur provides a factual account of the positive impact of integrated arts experiences upon a troubled student.

Oddliefson, E. (1989). *Music education as a gateway to improved academic performance in reading, math and science.* Washington, DC: CABC, The Center for Arts in the Basic Curriculum, Inc.

Oddliefson (CABC President) discusses the need for educational reform in the United States, citing declining scores in math and science. Several references are cited supporting the positive impact that music can have upon the development of academic skills.

*Oddliefson, E. (1991). *The arts as the vanguard to meaningful restructuring of the public school.* Keynote address to the Washington State Arts Education Action Plan Forum, Seattle, Washington, April 30, 1991.

The author argues that arts are the basis of school curricula, and he provides quotes from a variety of well known individuals in support of this claim. He concludes with a proposal for changing the school day so that the teaching of art consumes 30% (as compared to the present 10%) of the school day.

Oddliefson, E. (1990). The case for the arts. In *Context, 27,* 46–47.

Oddliefson makes a strong case for the arts as fundamental to learning and thinking processes in general. He discusses the "vertical" and "horizontal" aspects of the arts (arts as a stand-alone subject and arts infused with the other subjects) and how they promote both integrated learning and the education of the imagination.

*Oddliefson, E. (1992). *Exponential learning: A performance and results based educational system for the State of Washington.* Keynote address to the Washington Music Educators Association Biennial Convention, Tacoma, Washington, February 14, 1992.

The author brings together a number of references and quotations from well-known experts in the fields of education and the arts. The thesis of his talk is that the "President's educational goals for the year 2000 will not be achieved without the arts becoming required subjects along with other academic subjects in the curriculum" (p. 2).

*Ogbu, J. U. (1992). Adaptation to minority status and impact on school success. *Theory into Practice, 31* (4), 287–95.

This paper examines community forces underlying the educational problems of African Americans and other voluntary and involuntary minorities.

*Ogbu, J. U., & Simons, H. D. (1994). Cultural models of school achievement: A quantitative test of Ogbu's theory. *Cultural models of literacy: A comparative study* (Project 12). (ERIC Document Reproduction Service No. 376 515)

This study examined differences between cultural models and educational strategies of three minority groups (African Americans, Chinese Americans, and Mexican Americans/Latinos) to help explain differences in school performance. Results indicated that involuntary minorities (minorities incorporated into United States' society against their will through slavery or conquest) were more concerned with prejudice and discrimination, were less willing to conform to the dominant society's norms in order to succeed, were more concerned that crossing cultural boundaries would harm their social identity, and were less willing to conform to schools' expectations for good students than were voluntary minorities (minorities that chose to come to the United States).

*Opuni, K. A., Tullis, R. J., & Sanchez, K. S. (Spring 1995). Beating the odds: A support program for at-risk students. *ERS Spectrum, 13* (2), 37–43.

The authors describe the "Beating the Odds" (BTO) program that was initiated by the Houston Independent School District in the 1988–89 school year. The following recommendations resulted from the evaluation data (scores, attendance, statistics, etc.)

from the third year of the program:

- Improve teacher attitudes and knowledge about the program

- Implement a summer program (too much was lost while students were out of school during summer break)

- Provide in-services for teachers and other school staff

- Provide in-services for social workers

- Provide adequate space and telephone resources

- Provide incentives for parents (parental involvement is crucial!)

- Require principals to apply for participation in the program (it is important for administrators to demonstrate commitment to the program)

- Provide incentives and enrichment activities for students

Patrick, L. (1989, Fall). The importance of how we teach: An overview of modality strengths as related to general music instruction. *General Music Today, 3* (1), 4–6.

This article urges music teachers to combine auditory, visual, and tactile modes of learning in their lesson planning. Younger learners start as auditory and tactile learners.

*Patton, R. H., et. al. (1991). *Addressing the needs of St. Louis children at risk* (A report to the community from Project Respond, ED 338331). St. Louis: Missouri University, Public Policy Research Centers.

The report describes models of programs addressing the needs of poor, at-risk children.

Pearson, L. C., & Banerji, M. (1993). Effects of a ninth-grade dropout prevention program on student academic achievement, school attendance, and dropout rate. *The Journal of Experimental Education, 61,* 247–256.

The purpose of this study was to describe a dropout prevention program for ninth-grade students and examine its effects on grade point average, reading and math achievement, school attendance, and dropout rate. A random sample of ninth-grade students was drawn from six high schools for each of the three years that the program was in operation and was compared with a sample of students in the year prior to the program. Analysis of the program services across the school district revealed an emphasis on helping the students with academics and study skills. Significant positive effects were found on school attendance and dropout rate.

Perrin, S. (1989). Integrating arts and academics: An evolving model. In *Proceedings of the Symposium on the Importance of Music in Education* (pp. 28–35). Duxbury, MA: South Shore Conservatory.

Perrin points out the need to encourage imagination in schools.

Pezzullo, J. A. (1984). A comparison of study: Habits and attitudes among school dropouts and graduates in the Richmond, Indiana, public schools during 1979–81 (Doctoral dissertation, The Union for Experimental Colleges and Universities, 1983). *Dissertation Abstracts International, 44,* 2096A.

This study attempted to measure and make comparisons among 48 graduates and 48 dropouts in the Richmond, Indiana Public Schools. Results indicated that positive attitudes from both students and parents promoted a feeling of wanting to complete high school.

Phelan, W. T. (1992). Building bonds to high school graduation: Dropout intervention with seventh and eighth graders. *Middle School Journal, 24* (2), 33–35.

A principal at a Lowell, Massachusetts, school collaborated with the University of Massachusetts-Lowell to develop a dropout intervention program for seventh and eighth grade students. Small classes met alternate Saturday mornings at the university. Additional field trips and two overnight weekends helped strengthen the bond between students and their school.

*Pilecki, T. (1989). The miracle of the South Bronx—The story of the St. Augustine School. In *Proceedings of the Symposium on the Importance of Music in Education* (pp. 36–44). Duxbury, MA: South Shore Conservatory.

> "It is the purpose of the arts, to enhance what we are already doing with these children, to help them find the beauty amid the rubble .... The abstraction of the arts enhances a child's imagination and thinking skills .... The beauty of this whole program is that the kid who is having a terrible problem in math can maybe find that part of [himself or herself] to have something to be happy about, by being involved in an arts program, be it art or drama, or dance or music ...."

*Presseisen, B. Z. (Ed.). (1988). *At-risk students and thinking: Perspectives from research.* Washington, DC/Philadelphia, PA: A joint publication of the National Education Association and Research for Better Schools.

Pridgeon, M. P. (1982). The impact of the Florida alternative education act of 1978 as it related to dropouts, disciplinary actions and funding (Doctoral dissertation, Florida State University, 1981). *Dissertation Abstracts International, 42,* 4238A.

> This study was conducted to provide a formative evaluation of alternative education in Florida with respect to disciplinary actions, dropouts, and funding since enactment of the Alternative Education Act of 1978.

*Ratliff, M. (1991). St. Petersburg, Florida challenge: A school for at-risk students. In R. C. Morris & N. Schultz (Eds.), *A resource guide for working with youth at risk, vol. II* (pp. 126–129). Lancaster, PA: Technomic Publishing Company, Inc.

> Ratliff describes the Challenge School, an alternative school designed to increase at-risk students' self-esteem, academic achievement, and social/family functioning.

*Rauscher, F. (1994, September 6). Skills boost is music to parents' ears. *Fayetteville Observer Times,* p. F1.

> Twenty-two preschoolers (3-year-olds) were given weekly keyboard lessons that lasted 10 to 15 minutes, plus daily supervised practice. After only a few months, these children improved greatly on tests of spatial reasoning (matching puzzle pieces to a mental image). These children performed better than another group of children (same age) who did not have the music lessons.

Raywid, M. A. (1987). Excellence and choice: Friends or foes? *The Urban Review, 19* (1), 35–47.

> The "excellence" and "choice" school reform movements are discussed and compared. Special attention is focused on the at-risk student.

Reed, J. S. (1987). An investigation of compensatory education as a dropout intervention program for academically at-risk students in the elementary grades (Doctoral dissertation, University of Southern California, 1987). *Dissertation Abstracts International, 48,* 846A.

> This study was conducted to investigate the effectiveness of compensatory education to improve the achievement of moderate and high academic risk students in reading, mathematics, and language over a two-year period.

Reina, J. M. (1986). Fourth grade SRA scores as predictors of high school dropouts (Doctoral dissertation, University of Virginia, 1986). *Dissertation Abstracts International, 48,* 2854.

> The purpose of this study was to determine if an efficient and effective method of early identification of potential dropout students could be based on a standardized instrument. Scores obtained by 140 rural Virginia students, equally divided between male and female graduates and dropouts, showed correlation existed between all the SRA tests and graduation status.

Reahm, D. E. (1991). National Symposium on America's culture at risk. *Sforzando, 3* (4), 1, 6–8.

Sforzando is a publication of the Michigan Music Educators Association. Douglas Reahm is MMEA past president. This is a short description of the National Symposium and includes some interesting statistics.

Reitzammer, A. F. (1991). Dropout prevention: The early years. *Reading Improvement, 28* (4), 255–256.

This report urges dropout intervention during the early years of schooling, because children who are most likely to drop out of school are poorer readers than their peers and have repeated one or more grades. It is suggested that reading teachers carefully select instructional strategies and build students' self-esteem.

Robitaille, J. P., & O'Neal, S. (1981). Why instrumental music in elementary schools? *Phi Delta Kappan, 213.*

The researchers compared scores on the Comprehensive Tests of Basic Skills for 5154 students in 1979 and 5299 students in 1980. Consistently, students enrolled in band or orchestra scored higher. Students who had participated in instrumental music for two or more years ranked higher than nonparticipants in reading and language by 12 to 20 percentile. One-year participants also scored higher than nonparticipants.

Rogeau, J. L. (1989). Factors related to high school dropouts of a selected district in the State of Louisiana before and after a mandated curriculum. *Dissertation Abstracts International, 50,* 2376A.

Participation in extracurricular activities did not change before and after the mandate for either persisters or dropouts.

*Rosenkoetter, S. & Shotts, C. (1994). Bridging Early Services Transition Project-Outreach. Final Report. (ERIC Document Reproduction Service No. ED378 753)

The Bridging Early Services Transition Project-Outreach was designed to help families, administrators, and service providers facilitate the transition of young children, birth through age 5, as they move between services and service systems.

*Rumberger, R. W. (1983). Dropping out of high school: The influence of race, sex, and family background. *American Educational Research Journal, 20* (2), pp. 199–220.

Rumberger examined the extent of the high school dropout problem in 1979 and investigated both the stated reasons students leave school and some of the underlying factors influencing their decision. Attention was focused on differences by sex, race, and family background.

Rumberger, R. W. (1987). High school dropouts: A review of issues and evidence. *Review of Educational Research, 57* (2), 101–121.

Some of the elements needed to develop a successful strategy of dropout prevention and recovery include: (1) different programs designed for different types of dropouts, (2) an appropriate mix of educational and noneducational services in each program, (3) accurate and timely identification of students with a high risk of dropping out, and (4) programs designed for early prevention, late prevention, and recovery.

Sadowski, A. J. (1987). A case study of the experiences of and influences upon gifted high school dropouts (Doctoral dissertation, University of Miami, 1987). *Dissertation Abstracts International, 48,* 893A.

This study was developed to examine the social background, educational experiences, and psychological background of gifted high school dropouts. Recommendations included informing parents of their child's specific social, academic, and psychological problems; and providing courses and optional programs that meet the student's needs.

Sappington, J. P. (1981). The predictive strength of nine school-related indicators for distinguishing potential dropouts (Doctoral dissertation, United States International University,

1979). *Dissertation Abstracts International, 41,* 2944A.

> The purpose of this study was to determine if an
> objective process could be developed which would
> allow for the early identification of the dropout.
> Analysis of data indicated that dropouts could be dis-
> criminated from persisters at all grade levels; that
> dropouts could be predicted at the ninth, sixth, and
> fourth grades; and that at an early age it was feasible
> to predict whether a subject would drop out of school
> with an accuracy of 79% or greater.

*Schlimme, R. L. (1990). *Robert E. Lee Elementary School.*
Newsletter distributed by the Robert E. Lee Elementary
School, Columbia, MO 65201.

> This newsletter describes positive influences of arts
> upon student motivation and achievement.

Scripp, L., & Meyaard, J. (1991). Encouraging musical risks
for learning success. *Music Educators Journal, 78* (3), 36–41.

> These case studies of at-risk students and music
> describe how SongSmith, a computer composition
> tool, helped motivate students.

*Schwartz, W. (1995). *School programs and practices for
homeless students* (Digest Number 105); *School dropouts:
New information about an old problem* (Digest Number 109).
[On-line]. Available from: http://eric-web.tc.columbia.edu/
home_files/eric_cue_desc.htm/

*Shuler, S. C. (1991). Music, at-risk students, and the missing
piece. *Music Educators Journal, 78* (3), 21–29.

> Instruction should be suited to the learning style of the
> student, and that style may include using musical
> intelligence (i.e., Gardner, 1985). Shuler explains how
> music may help the at-risk student learn and describes
> at-risk programs that use music.

Simner, M. L., & Barnes, M. J. (1991, Winter). Relationship
between first-grade marks and the high school dropout problem. *Journal of School Psychology, 29,* 331–5.

This study found evidence for the possibility of early identification through school performance indicators.

Sipe, C., Grossman, J., & Milliner, J. (1988). *Summer training and education program (STEP): Report on the 1987 experience.* Philadelphia: Public/Private Ventures.

Public/Private Ventures is a nonprofit research and program development agency for youth services. Results of projects indicate the need for intensive intervention programs for high-risk youth providing educational enrichment, job training, and focusing on increasing sexual responsibility.

*Sizer, T. (1984). *Horace's compromise: The dilemma of the American high school.* Boston: Houghton-Mifflin.

Renewed public attention to the importance of teaching in high schools and to the complexity and subtlety of the teaching craft is urged. Without good teachers, sensibly deployed, schooling is barely worth the effort. High schools exist not merely to subject the pupils to brute training ... but to develop their powers of thought, of taste, and of judgment.

Slicker, E. K., & Palmer, D. J. (1993). Mentoring at-risk high school students: Evaluation of a school-based program. *The School Counselor, 40,* 327–334.

In this study, school personnel were trained tutors. Contains descriptions of mentoring behaviors.

Smartschan, G. F. (1979). An evaluation of an alternative program for potential dropouts in the Allentown school district (Doctoral dissertation, Lehigh University, 1979). *Dissertation Abstracts International, 40-03A,* 1398.

Analysis of data indicated that students in the Allentown program made significant gains on a standardized reading test and a standardized mathematics test during their enrollment in the On-Site Center. The number of failing grades received on report cards also decreased.

Smyer, R., & Bliss, K. (1991). *Crockett's Project Success: 1990–91 evaluation report, executive summary.* Austin Independent School District, TX: Office of Research and Evaluation.

This report describes an evaluation of Project Success, a dropout prevention program at Crockett High School in Austin, Texas. At-risk ninth graders (103 students) were involved in the project, and these students were compared with a similar group at another school. The findings are discussed, and statistical data are included.

Soderburg, L. J. (1988). Educators' knowledge of the characteristics of high school dropouts. *High School Journal, 71* (3), 108–115.

Dropouts tend to not be involved in extracurricular activities.

*Spencer, W. A., & Bearden, L. J. (1987). *The high school dropout: Findings from 400 interviews with dropouts in Alabama.* Paper presented at the Annual Meeting of the American Educational Studies Association, Chicago, IL.

Dropouts were interviewed about why they dropped out. The article also provides descriptions of the dropout, economic effects of dropping out, and opinions of educational reform.

Spiegel, R. A. (1988). *Computers and the Waterways Project* (The Waterways Project, 799 Greenwich Street, New York, NY). Paper presented at the Conference of the New York State Association for Computers and Technology.

The paper describes how its clientele (students with drug problems, high school dropouts, and youth in transition) gained the encouragement to try to have their literary work published, which is intended to give them direction. The project also was involved with book fairs, computer programming, a literary arts publishing program, and adult poetry workshops.

*Stallings, J. (1987). Longitudinal findings for early childhood programs: Focus on direct instruction. The Lipman Papers:

Appropriate Programs for Four-Year-Olds. (ERIC Document
Reproduction Service No. ED 29787)

> Based on the premise that positive reinforcement is
> essential to maximum academic success, the Direct
> Instruction program was developed from an academic
> preschool model specifying exactly what children
> needed in order to succeed academically and dictated
> how teachers should modify children's behavior.

The state plan to reduce the dropout rate. (1991). Texas
Education Agency. Austin, TX: Publications distribution
office, Texas Education Agency, 1701 North Congress Avenue,
Austin, TX. (ERIC Document Reproduction Service No. ED
338757)

> The Texas plan advises teacher renewal, minority
> recruitment, attention to learning styles, individualized
> attention, smaller schools and classes, flexible sched-
> ules, multiage elementary classes, mentorships, and
> empowerment.

*Statement of beliefs. (1991, May). *Issues in Music Education,*
p. 3. Reston, VA: Music Educators National Conference.

> This document simply lists MENC's 78 "Statement of
> Beliefs," which are excellent guidelines and rationale
> for providing music experiences for every student at
> all grade levels.

Stephens, R. T., & Repa, J. T. (1992). Dropping out and its
ultimate consequence: A study of dropouts in prison. *Urban
Education, 26* (4), 401–422.

> The study compared 220 adult male felons incarcerat-
> ed in New York State's Sing Sing Correctional facility
> (79% were dropouts and 84% were from urban set-
> tings) to dropouts described in the literature. The
> dropouts had many similarities with nonincarcerated
> dropouts and had more in common with them than
> with fellow inmates.

*Stief, E. (1994). Transitions to school. (ERIC Document
Reproduction Service No. ED 377974)

Short- and long-term outcomes of the Direct
Instruction Head Start and Follow Through program
model are reported. This program was based on the
premise that positive reinforcement is essential to
maximum academic success.

Stokrocki, M. (1989, Spring). *Suggestions for teaching art to
at-risk students* (Report distributed by the NAEA Advisory of
the National Art Education Association). Reston, VA: National
Art Education Association.

School attributes that contribute to the production of
dropouts include the need for high teacher expectations, cooperative learning, individualization, a sense
of responsibility, relevance, social aspects, competi-
tions. References about dropouts, teaching reading
through art, and effective dropout programs are
included.

Stories of hope & courage through art (1993, May). *American
Artist, 57,* 59.

Learning through Art is an organization that offers
workshops in helping teach low-income urban children to read and write. Public school teachers work
with artists to relate language development with art
creation. Learning through Art also has programs for
at-risk children and for special needs children. More
information is available from Learning through Art,
The Guggenheim Museum Children's Program, Dept.
AA, 1071 Fifth Avenue, New York, NY 10128.

*Strother, D. B. (1987). Dropping out. *Phi Delta Kappan,*
325–28.

Circumstances contributing to a student's decision to
drop out of school are discussed.

*Strother, D. B. (Ed.). (1991) *Learning to fail: Case studies of
students at risk.* Bloomington, IN: Phi Delta Kappa, Maynard
R. Bemis Center for Evaluation, Development, and Research.

Vivid portrayals of students at risk point out the individual nature of the "at-risk" phenomenon. Several of

the students reported in these cases reported talent and interest in the arts, often the only thing they enjoyed about school.

Surace, E. (1992). Everyone wants to join the chorus. *Phi Delta Kappan,* 608–612.

Arts programs can be true learning experiences for all children, combining language and social skills and allowing them to fulfill themselves.

Swisher, K., & Hoisch, M. (January, 1992). Dropping out among American Indians and Alaska natives: A review of studies. *Journal of American Indian Education, 31,* 3–23.

A review of research into dropout rates and reasons for dropping out among American Indians and Alaska natives.

*Taylor, J. A. (1993). A survey of drop-out and at-risk programs in music. Unpublished report, Center for Music Research, Florida State University.

*Taylor, J. A., & Anderson, T. (1993). *Multicultural arts education: Guidelines, instructional units and resources for art, dance, music, and theater, Grades K–12.* Tallahassee, FL: Florida Department of Education.

Definitions and the goals of multicultural education are offered, along with results of a survey of multicultural arts instruction in Florida. Specific guidelines for the development of multicultural instructional units are listed, and seven model instructional units are presented in the four arts areas. An extensive listing of resources for creating units in various world cultures concludes this practical manual.

*Taylor, J. A., & Davis, B. (1996). A survey of at-risk prevention programs in Florida. Unpublished manuscript, Center for Music Research, Florida State University.

*Thompson, J. T. (1991). Establishing locus of control among ninth graders: Using peer mentors to reduce student disengagement, absenteeism, and failures. Nova University, FL:

EdD Practicum, 67 pp. (ERIC Document Reproduction
Service No. ED 337738)

Bibliography

Student attendance and grades were improved by pair-
ing eleventh graders with ninth graders.

Titone, J. S. (1979). Educational strategies for preventing stu-
dents from dropping out of high school (Doctoral dissertation,
Claremont Graduate School, 1979). *Dissertation Abstracts
International, 35,* 6458A.

This study explored three educational strategies that
have been used to help students reduce their academic
failures. One strategy concerned methods for improving reading skills, the second strategy involved a program of computer identification, and the third strategy
was an innovative experimental achievement program.
Academic progress, over a two-year period, was moni-
tored for both the experimental and control groups.
Each group significantly reduced their number of "F"
grades, but no significant differences were found
among groups.

Trusty, J., & Dooley-Dickey, K. (1991). *At-risk students: A
profile for early identification.* Paper presented at the Annual
Convention of the American Association of counseling and
Development, Reno, NV.

Examines available information on early identification
of students at risk of prematurely dropping out of
school. A variety of factors were found to be predictors, and it is recommended that a means of early
identification of potential dropout students be developed. Suggestions are made regarding approaches that
may be taken to develop these early profiles.

Tsurutome, S. M. (1987). *Profile of a dropout.* A report from
the Institute for Research and development in Teacher
Education, College of Education, Boca Raton, FL: Florida
Atlantic University.

This report describes characteristics and circumstances
associated with students who drop out of school.

*United States Department of Labor, The Secretary's Commission on Achieving Necessary Skills. (1992). *Learning a living: A blueprint for high performance. A SCANS report for America 2000.* Washington, DC: U. S. Government Printing Office.

*United States General Accounting Office. (1987). *School dropouts: Survey of local programs.* (GAO publication No. HRD-87-108). Washington, DC: United States General Accounting Office, Human Resources Division.

> The information in this report is based largely on responses to a mail survey from administrators of 479 local dropout programs that were in operation in the 1985–86 school year and were reported continuing in 1986–87, and on visits to 14 dropout programs. The survey's results provide information about programs perceived as effective by local administrators.

United States General Accounting Office. (1986). *School dropouts: The extent and nature of the problem.* (GAO Publication No. HRD-86-106BR). Washington, DC: United States General Accounting Office, Briefing Report to Congressional Requesters.

> Factors related to dropping out of school include higher dropout rates for Hispanics, blacks, and youth from households of lower socioeconomic status. Youth drop out of school for family, school, and work-related reasons. Being behind grade level is one of the most powerful predictors for dropping out. Self-reported reasons for dropping out include poor grades, not liking school, marriage or marriage plans, pregnancy, and preference or need for work. Since self-reporting can be influenced by youth's perceptions of their circumstances, it may not provide completely accurate profiles.

Walker, B. C. (1980). The relative effect of painting and cross-motor activities on the intrinsic locus-of-control of hyperactivity in learning disabled elementary school pupils. *Studies in Art Education, 21* (2), 13–21.

> This study found that painting and gross motor activity increased attention almost by a factor of two.

Walker, S., et al. (1982). *Title I children's program: Learning to read through the arts* (Final evaluation report, 1981–82). Brooklyn, NY: New York City Board of Education, Office of Educational Evaluation.

This report presents a brief program description and results of an evaluation of student achievement and teacher participation in 1981–82 of Learning to Read through the Arts, which offers intensive reading instruction to New York City elementary school students, through the integration of a total arts program with a total reading program.

Washington State Johnson O'Malley Indian Education 1983–84 Annual Report (1984). Olympia, WA: Washington Office of the State Superintendent of Public Instruction.

The overall objectives of the program described included increase reading and math proficiency, improve the high school graduation rate, promote cultural and ethnic awareness activities, and increase participation in extracurricular activities. Evaluation showed mean achievement points in reading and 5.8 points in math over 1983 scores. The high school dropout rate was 1.7% compared with 13% in 1983. Indian students participated in various activities including student government, band, and athletics.

*Watson, K. (1991). Comprehensive at-risk education: Making a difference in children's lives. In R. C. Morris & N. Schultz (Eds.). *A resource guide for working with youth at risk, vol. II* (pp. 109–110). Lancaster, PA: Technomic Publishing Company, Inc.

The Comprehensive At-Risk Education (CARE) project is described.

*Wehlage, G., Lipman, P., & Smith, G. (1989). *Empowering communities for school reform: The Annie E. Casey Foundation's New Future Initiative.* Madison: Wisconsin Center for Education Research.

The authors support empowering faculty and staff to make appropriate decisions for each school site.

*Wehlage, G. G., Rutter, R. A., & Turnbaugh, A. (1987). A program model for at-risk high school students. *Educational Leadership 44* (6): 70–73.

An innovative program for at-risk students is presented.

*West Virginia School Dropout Prevention Task Force. (1991). In class, in step: A community resource guide for school dropout prevention. Charleston, WV: State Department of Education. (ERIC Document Reproduction Service No. ED 330941)

This article reports that 93% of dropouts in West Virginia never participated in extracurricular activities. Behaviors that place students at risk and proactive strategies for teachers are also presented, and the roles of both the school and the community are discussed.

*Wilcynski, M. M. (1987). A study to determine the feasibility of identifying potential high school dropouts in elementary school (Doctoral dissertation, University of Iowa, 1986). *Dissertation Abstracts International, 47,* 2378A.

Characteristics of two groups, dropouts and graduates, were studied to determine the significant differences between the groups in areas of demographics, students' behaviors, and academic achievement/intellectual abilities. There were significant differences between the two groups in 18 of the 20 selected characteristics.

*Wilson, M. M. B. (1985). Early school withdrawals: An exploratory survey of preferences for solutions from teachers, counselors, administrators, and dropouts (Doctoral dissertation, George Peabody College for Teachers of Vanderbilt University, 1985). *Dissertation Abstracts International, 46,* 1598A.

This study explored the preferences of administrators, teachers, counselors, and school dropouts regarding possible solutions for decreasing the dropout problem in a rural Tennessee county public school system via a questionnaire. Data indicated that (1) positive peer influence, (2) helping students feel success, (3) placing greater emphasis on reading problems in elementary school, and (4) providing additional information from Planned Parenthood were preferences of the four groups surveyed.

Winborne, D. G. (1991). *Affective education for at-risk students: The view of urban principals.* Paper presented at the 1991 Annual Meeting of the American Educational Research Association, Chicago, IL.

This study suggests that any alternative program for at-risk students within an urban school district must have a strong affective component. Affective dimensions of student development appeared to have high importance in the minds of principals who participated in the survey.

Wohl, S. F. (1973). Benjamin Franklin Street Academy (Function No. 09-39614). Brooklyn, NY: New York City Board of Education.

Students selected for the program were potential high school dropouts with educational deficiencies of two or more years in reading and in mathematics. Also, they had a record of failed courses, high absence, truancy and negative attitudes toward school and self. In addition to extensive tutoring, the program offered instruction in English, reading, writing, mathematics, Spanish, history, contemporary issues, chemistry, psychology, music (elective) and videotaping (elective).

Wolf, T., & Wolf, D. P. (1985). The arts as reinforcers of basic academic skills. *Education Digest, 51,* 44–55.

The authors claim that arts participation improves skills of observation, reasoning, reading, studying, and mathematics.

Wright, E. N., and Young, R. E. (1986). *Arts in education. The use of drama and narrative: A study of outcomes.* Toronto: Ontario Department of Education.

The report studied a drama program presented by three visiting drama consultants and a daily story-reading period presented by the teacher. It suggested that the daily use of stories or the use of drama contributes to academic achievement. Results indicated a greater chance for demonstrable benefits in academic achievement with story-telling than with drama and that the chances for demonstrable benefits are greater with inner-city children.

Yagi, K. (1987). *ECIA, Chapter I Early Childhood Education Program in the Portland Public Schools, 1986–87 Evaluation Report.* Portland, OR: Public Schools, Research and Evaluation Department.

The preschool curriculum included language, mathematics, small and large motor functions, art and music, and personal and social development. Many techniques replicated those of the Headstart Program and the Montessori method. Data indicate that the program helps children master skills and that replication of the program across years has produced consistent results.

*You gotta have art (1991, April 17). *USA Today,* 7A-9A.

This is a special feature of the value of the arts to minorities and at-risk children. Included are testimonials by Ben Vereen, Wynton Marsalis, Charles Schultz, Garth Williams, Shelley Duvall, and Jean Kennedy Smith. A number of arts magnet schools are briefly described, and narratives of success stories in the arts are presented.